BROKE IS BEAUTIFUL

Living and Loving the Cash-Strapped Life

BY LAURA LEE

RUNNING PRESS

PHILADELPHIA · LONDON

9 8 7 6 5 4 3 2 1

Digit on the right indicates the number of this printing

Library of Congress Control Number: 2009941871

ISBN 978-0-7624-3895-2

Cover and interior design by Jason Kayser

Edited by Jennifer Kasius

Typography: Chronicle, Clarendon, and Whitney

Cover photo (wallet): © iStockphoto.com/Grigoriy Lukyanov

Cover photo (gold card): © iStockphoto.com/Jared DeCinque

Running Press Book Publishers
2300 Chestnut Street
Philadelphia, PA 19103-4371

Visit us on the web!
www.runningpress.com

THERE is no such thing as independence, only interdependence. This book is dedicated to my late father, author Albert Lee, from whom I stole that line. To my brother and unofficial research assistant, Dr. Christopher (Cal) Lee. To my mother, Carol Lee, for providing a home and safe haven during my financially insecure times. To Valery Lantratov for inspiration and international perspective. To my life-long friend Jennifer Hunter for on-going moral support in richer and poorer times. To my wonderful new agent Laura Ross (Lauras rule!) for believing a book with a target audience of "broke people" could sell.

Thank you to editor Jennifer Kasius for making me sound more articulate than I do in normal life. Thanks to copyeditor Erin Slonaker and designer Jason Kayser.

A Big Thanks to the "Social Network Team," the folks who offered me tips and suggestions during the writing of this book: Richard Allman, Ken Boullt, Lisa Bruno, Lisa Crawford, Jodi Connors-Bergman, Jacqueline Clapper, Sandra Deering, Daniel Gill, Kristin Hertz, Valorie Howard, Shane Hunter, Dianne Ilkka, Nancy Jones, John Longo, Marlin McCoy, Gary McKeever, Larry Mein, Thane Norton, Jodi Prahler, Lynda Pringle, Bonnie Ray, Tanya Roycraft, Pat Salzer, Sue Schier, Helen Stewart, Sarah Stewart

And praise be to librarians everywhere! I bow down at your feet.

Contents

....

Introduction:
I Was Broke Before
It Was Cool!

"For the love of money is the root of all evil: which while some coveted after, they have erred from the faith, and pierced themselves through with many sorrows."

—1 TIMOTHY 6:10

For years I've been jealous of the folks who lived during the Great Depression. Sure there were bread lines and people were out of work, but they had those great union songs to make the poor folk feel powerful: "You can't scare me, I'm sticking with the union!" They had sad songs to make the poor folk feel sympathy: "Once I built a railroad, made it run, made it race against time." They even had escapist songs so that poor folk could fantasize: "We're in the money, we're in the money." The poor were the subject of art and literature, from the portraits of Dorothea Lange to the novels of John Steinbeck.

You may have been broke, and life may have been hard, but you got a lot of sympathy. You and your modest means were part of the culture. There was a sense that people were all in it together.

I came of age in the Reagan era, watching videos of the Duran boys swanning around on boats in exotic locations and Madonna singing "Material Girl." We watched Alex P. Keaton in *Family Ties* and Gordon Gekko in the movie *Wall Street*. The grubby rustic hippies were *so* last decade. They started trusting people over thirty, put on suits, and became Yuppies. They wanted everyone to know about their new-found hobby of building up wealth.

Shows began to pop up on television that equated poor fashion sense with moral failing. We drooled at *Lifestyles of the Rich and Famous*. Our culture focused on flipping houses, redecorating their interiors, and watching Silicon Valley tech geeks become millionaires. Sure, there were lots of people building up crushing debt, but it wasn't something we talked about—or even thought about if we didn't have to. (Heck, those debts hadn't crushed anybody yet.) We had easy credit. Our home values were going up and up, so we'd have more tomorrow than today. Spend now—or the terrorists win!

Dale Wasserman, the playwright who created *Man of La Mancha*, described himself as a "showbiz hobo." I am a literary and theatrical hobo. I have pieced together a living writing books, organizing ballet tours, and taking odd jobs like shopping mall Easter Bunny and clerk at The Arlozone, a combination Arlo Guthrie merchandise store and coffee shop in Pittsfield, Massachusetts. (I was as shocked as anyone when the place went out of business.)*

---

* *If it seems that there are a few more references to Arlo and Woody Guthrie than you would necessarily expect in this book, it stems back to the years I worked at the Arlozone and as a volunteer at Arlo Guthrie's community organization, The Guthrie Center.*

My economic station has seen me rolling quarters to make my rent and looking up dandelion recipes on the Internet to make use of a free crop that appeared in the lawn. Nevertheless, I kept having to buy food—it threw off my whole budget. I was completely out of style.

Nowadays, I feel like the ugly duckling who has grown into a swan. I see that I was a trendsetter, ahead of the curve. Now everybody is talking about what they can't afford. They're discussing gas prices, mortgage payments, and their grocery bills. Doing more with less is the new black. I can stand up and say, "I was broke before it was cool—and broke can be beautiful!"

So welcome, wealthless, and congratulations on coming out of the closet. Never has there been a better time to hold your head high as a cash-strapped person. When once you were on your own, being told to pull yourself up by your bootstraps, today you're part of a movement!

President John F. Kennedy said that "a rising tide raises all boats." It is also true that a lowering tide brings the boat back down to the folks who have been treading water. Since I've been here for a while, I want you to know that the water here is fine. I feel that I am more than qualified to guide all of you who have suddenly realized your fortune was part of a "bubble" on the joys of being broke. Yes, I said the *joys* of being broke. It helps if you can look on your poverty as a way to lighten your load and a chance to test your creativity and resourcefulness. You might as well look at it that way anyhow, because you're still going to be broke either way.

The premise of this book is simple: Being broke is not abnormal. Being rich, on the other hand, is freakish. This will not be a how-to guide on dealing with a tight budget or simple living, although some of those types of tips will slip in here and there. It is a mental guide for keeping your sanity in troubled times by seeing your poverty from different perspectives—economic, historic, and cultural.

Not everyone sees money the way we're accustomed to in our culture. Seeing yourself as an irresponsible lazy bum is only one option, and if you're suffering financial reverses, it's probably not the best one for your well-being. Try one of these alternatives on for size: Consider yourself an eco-savvy member of the green movement, a spiritually evolved person who has given up materialism, or a resourceful artist of life. Remember that the word *wealth* comes from the Old English weal, which means well-being. Being wealthy simply means you're doing well, so you don't need money to pull it off.

If you're contemplating being flat-out busted for the first time after a period of prosperity, chances are you're only thinking about the negatives. Daniel Gilbert, a noted happiness researcher (one of those job titles you never knew existed), points out that things that we anticipate will give us joy make us less happy than we think, and things that fill us with dread will make us less unhappy, for less long, than we think.

Just as buying that dream house didn't make you as happy as you'd imagined, having it foreclosed for non-payment won't make you feel as bad as you imagine. I'm not saying it won't be embarrassing and that you won't feel bad about it. But that shame won't be the only thing in your life; you'll still have your friends and your thoughts and your talents, and you'll still have happy days. What's more, when something you thought would ruin you happens and you're still standing, you tend to feel a lot more resilient and strong. I know, I've had lots of time to think about this stuff. I was broke before it was cool.

2

Planning Tips for a Successful Life of Poverty

"I don't think McDonald's is necessarily a bad place to work, but I wouldn't say that's the only alternative for people who are trained in banking."

—PAUL HAZEN, CHAIRMAN OF WELLS FARGO & CO. (RESPONDING TO A QUESTION ON RETRAINING THOUSANDS OF FIRED EMPLOYEES IN 1996.)

Greetings, *nouveau pauvre*. If you're planning now to be broke, congratulations! You're in a great position to lay the groundwork for a successful transition. My personal recommendation (from the "do as I say" file) is to pursue the debt-free approach to being poor. In this lifestyle you don't have much to show for yourself, but you aren't shooing away creditors either.

Even though it has been the "done thing" in America for some time, being in a state of obligation comes with more than just cash flow hassles. Psychologists and sociologists tell us that reciprocal arrangements are so vital in human social systems that we are essentially programmed to feel uncomfortable when we are in a position to receive but not to give. What's more, other people dislike us as well if we break this unwritten rule of reciprocity. Your friend may say she doesn't mind picking up the tab when you go out to lunch, but she minds. And you know she minds.

In fact, most people will avoid asking for help when they need it if they know they're not in a position to pay the favor back. The psychological cost may outweigh the material loss.

If you can plan ahead to avoid this, you can avoid what I call the Elvis Effect. You may remember that Elvis was famous for his over-the-top generosity. In his most famous spending spree, he gave away brand-new cars to his friends and a woman who just happened to be in the dealership at the time. When someone acts that way, you can bet that he used to be poor. That is a person trying to balance the scales in a big way for the time that he was down.

The person who says everyone should pull himself up by his bootstraps, on the other hand, probably didn't have as far to pull.* A person who feels this way is more likely to have been born with social advantages that he takes for granted, and to view all of his success as self-made.

This is not to say that the poor are morally superior. That would be as absurd as the notion that the rich are morally superior. There are simply underlying psychological and social reasons why people act as they do.

Knowing this in advance, you can prepare yourself by creating your own psychological safety valve. If most of your socializing

---

*Booting *a computer is related to pulling yourself up by your bootstraps. In the early days, the initial bit of program code was called a "bootstrap loader," a reference to the lifting feat. This was soon abbreviated first to* bootstrap *and then to* boot.

revolves around spending—going to movies, going out to eat—you're going to start feeling like a mooch and cut yourself off from other people.

Studies show that people who feel financially strapped are much less socially engaged than those who feel more secure. Adjusting for income and education, the most financially stressed attend two-thirds fewer meetings of clubs and organizations than the least economically anxious. The broke not only go to movies less frequently (they can't afford it), but they also spend less time on things that don't cost a cent, like having friends over, going to visit friends, attending church, volunteering, and participating in politics. The only thing financial stress seems to make us do more of is watch TV. Such social isolation can easily lead to clinical depression, which further isolates and makes it harder to engage in the kind of productive, creative thoughts that can lead to novel solutions to your problems.

So you have to be proactive and do the inviting. Come up with cheery free stuff to do, and you suggest the activity. Have a potluck. Plan a scavenger hunt. Have a bird-watching outing. If you do it early and often, your friends will think of you as a creative person who suggests out-of-the-ordinary activities, and they'll actually feel more positive about you.

Social activities do not have to be extravagant; they just need to be done together. Philip Simmons, author of *Learning to Fall*, gets nostalgic when he's around garbage. "When I was spending summers [in New Hampshire] as a child, about the only time I got to spend with my father was while we were working together on something, and so I have fond memories of our trips to the dump. The work (of lugging trash to the dump) was tedious and smelly, and I don't suppose we talked a whole lot, but it was good simply to be in my father's presence . . ."

One thing that can isolate folks without money is a sense that your digs just aren't quite good enough for company. Think about this for a moment. Are you inviting them over to be impressed with you, or to be friends with you? Are they more likely to be impressed by your interest in what they have to say or by the slip covers on your chairs?

Alice Brock, the subject of folk singer Arlo Guthrie's Vietnam-era anthem "Alice's Restaurant," published her own cookbook in 1969. If you have a soft spot for late '60s counter culture (you really ought to if you're broke), I highly recommend it. Alice offers the following advice on entertaining hippie style:

"Just because you have four chairs, six plates and three cups is no reason why you can't invite twelve people to dinner. There are lots of things you can use besides plates. For instance: hub caps lined with tinfoil, or almost anything lined with tinfoil . . ." The plastic tops of coffee can lids, empty jars, plastic yogurt and ice cream tubs, measuring cups, and baking pans all have potential as dishes. Alice recommends popsicle sticks and wire hangers as forks. "Also, any chance you get, take wooden ice cream spoons from the market. They're free." (Anyone seen those lately?) The key is serving with confidence and style.

"If you act embarrassed, you'll never be able to pull this kind of stunt off," she writes, "but if you're straight ahead and act like you always serve your Beef Stroganoff in a muffin tin, everybody will think you're very exciting and original and that maybe there's something *they* don't know."

Being broke with someone else is a great way to bond. You can prove this by watching just about any VH1 *Behind the Music* special ever made. If you haven't seen one, here is the plot: A group of working class kids from London/New York/Los Angeles/any economically depressed industrial city are drawn together by a dream of making it big in the music business, and they form a rock band. On the way up as they tour in a rusted van held together by duct tape they are the best of friends and share a far off dream of superstardom. Then one day they discover they have made it. They are showered with gold records and enough money to support whatever vice they wish to pursue. Without the struggle to make a living to unite them, things start to fall apart.

They begin to discover that they may not have had that much in common after all. The initial joy fizzles, the music suffers, they each blame the others, and the band breaks up. (That is until the money runs out and the members suddenly remember that they kind of liked each other to begin with and besides, that promoter sure is offering a lot of dosh for a summer reunion tour.)

Jon Moss, drummer for the 1980s band Culture Club, reflected on his group's implosion saying, "Generally, the more expensive the album, the less successful the band is becoming."

While we're talking about '80s music, you may also want to start humming the Janet Jackson song, "Control." (I was pleased to know there is someone in control, but I was a bit surprised that it is Janet

Jackson.) Study after study shows that people feel more relaxed, creative, and productive when they believe they are in control of their lives.

In *Stumbling on Happiness*, Daniel Gilbert reports on a study with dramatic results. Researchers gave each resident of a nursing home a houseplant. They told half of the elderly residents that they were in control of the plant's care and feeding. The other residents were told that a staff member would water the plant. The members were allowed to set the timing and duration of the student researcher's visit. The low-control group members were not. After two months, residents of the high-control group were happier, healthier, more productive, and taking fewer medications than the low-control group. Six months later, 30 percent of the residents in the low-control group had died compared with only 15 percent in the high control group. But the real revelation did not come until the study ended.

When the study was finished, the students went home. Several months later, they did a follow-up and were saddened to learn that a disproportionate number of the residents who had been in the high-control group had died. The residents had been given control, only to have it taken away when the study ended.

"Apparently," wrote Gilbert, "gaining control can have a positive impact on one's health and well-being, but losing control can be worse than never having any at all."

This explains the seemingly illogical fact that the first thing most people do when they get laid off is go out and buy something. "You see, I'm still in control, I can buy this toaster." In a consumer society, we tend to feel in control when we have access to lots of goods and services. Choosing between the eco-friendly recycled toilet paper and the novelty toilet paper with the crossword puzzles on it gives us a sense of control. The loss of a job is a serious blow to your ability to make those choices.

Once the unemployment runs out, you probably will lose control over your ability to get that toaster. But even though you have lost control in one area does not mean you have lost it in all areas. In fact, the sense that you ever had control was a bit of an illusion. No one is control of everything.

Will Rogers said, "We're all ignorant, only on different subjects." It is equally true that we are all in control, only in different areas. The key to maintaining a successful Broke and Beautiful lifestyle is to focus on what you do control, and not on what you cannot. In the pages that follow, we'll explore various ways to do just that.

A quick note on language: There is a shade of difference between the words "broke" and "poor." Broke generally refers to a temporary state of affairs, while poor is a more permanent social status. We talk about the "working poor" but not the "working broke," for example. Because the experience of rolling pennies to put enough gas in your car in order to get to work is the same whether you are "broke" or "poor," I will be using the two terms relatively interchangeably throughout this book.

What Is a Deadbeat?

How did a person who doesn't pull his own weight come to be known as a deadbeat? It goes all the way back to the Civil War. (The same war gave us the word deadline.) Back in those days people used the word beat to mean "swindle" or "cheat." So Civil War soldiers called the guy who shirked his duty a "beat." The worst kind of beat, and the most hated, was the guy who metaphorically played dead by faking a wound or illness to escape duty—a deadbeat. As so many of our ideas tend to do in America, the concept of the "deadbeat" drifted toward the economic in the years that followed.

A Cash-Strapped Life Is a Creative Life: The Adventure of Being Broke

"I also want to thank my parents in Vergaio, who gave me the greatest gift: poverty."

—ROBERTO BENIGNI, ON WINNING THE OSCARS FOR BEST ACTOR AND BEST FOREIGN FILM, 1999.

You probably knew someone like this in high school or college—he was a budding novelist who spent all his time scribbling in a notebook and talking about the great book he would write that would change how the world thought about literature. If you asked this guy what type of books he liked to read, he would tell you that he didn't read other writers because he didn't want to pollute his ground water. He couldn't care less how a bunch of dead poets did things. The past is dead and gone, your friend would say, and he was all about the future.

Several years have now passed, and I would be willing to bet one of two things about your "creative" friend. He has now either 1) started to read other writers or 2) given up on his writing dream and gotten a job in middle management.

One of the defining characteristics of creativity, of course, is novelty. We define something as creative if it has an element of innovation. But there are other aspects of creativity that are much less frequently discussed. Creativity is as much about *constraint* as it is about innovation. You could, for example, put a bunch of random words on the page, print them out, and call it poetry because those words have never appeared together in quite that configuration before. It would be somewhat original (I'm guessing it's been done), but it wouldn't mean much of anything to anyone. Most likely they wouldn't even recognize that it was supposed to be a poem. Knowing what has come before, and drawing on it, is a constraint, but it is a *useful* constraint.

Dr. Patricia Stokes studied artistic innovators such as Igor Stravinsky, Pablo Picasso, and Frank Lloyd Wright and determined that contrary to common belief, it is not complete freedom that leads to creative innovation. Successful artists move forward within self-imposed restrictions. Stokes calls these constraints "barriers that lead to breakthroughs."

Stokes makes a distinction between the kinds of constraints that invite conformity: "operators in well-structured problems with single correct solutions, like directions to memorize, calculate exactly, or copy correctly . . . preclude the surprising and promote the expected." Other types of structures and constraint, however, provide a foundation upon which a person can build and innovate. I'll illustrate this with my favorite limerick:

There once was a man from Japan
Who wrote verse that never would scan

When they said that the thing
Didn't go with the swing
He said, "Yes, but I always like to fit as many words into the last
line as I possibly can."

In her book, *Creativity from Constraints*, Stokes did not specifically address budget constraints, but I can assure you that trying to find a solution with limited capital can be just the kind of "barrier that leads to breakthroughs."

"There's lot's of freedom that comes from having less money," said Roger Hedden, writer and producer of such independent films as *Sleep with Me* and *Bodies, Rest and Motion*. "For the most part, the lack of money to throw at problems makes you come up with creative solutions. And in the end I think the project becomes better because you have a set of restrictions that are imposed that aren't imposed with an eye toward the marketplace, but are just constraints that you have to be creative around."

For ten years, Arnold M. Ludwig studied the lives of 1,004 men and women who were prominent in a variety of fields including art, music, science, sports, politics, and business. He published the results in the 1995 book *The Price of Greatness: Resolving the Creativity and Madness Controversy*. As part of his study, Ludwig identified a template for greatness. Among the traits of exceptional people were a sense of physical vulnerability and the existence of psychological "unease." What better to produce those two things than a little shot of poverty?

There was a time when the benefits of a pauper's life were common knowledge, as Malcolm Gladwell observed in *The New Yorker*: "The rags-to-riches story—that staple of American biography—has over the years been given two very different interpretations," he wrote. "The nineteenth-century version stressed the value of compensating for disadvantage. If you wanted to end up on top, the thinking went, it was better to start at the bottom, because it was there that you learned the discipline and motivation essential for success. . . . Today that interpretation has been reversed. Success is seen as a matter of capitalizing on socioeconomic advantage, not compensating for disadvantage. . . . Nowadays, we don't learn from poverty, we escape from poverty . . ."

If nothing else, having bills to pay can get you off your butt. When it comes to innovation, the profit motive has got nothing on the survival motive. The list of great works of art and literature that were created so the artist could make a buck to pay the rent or buy some bread is too long to list.

While poverty can be a great motivator to get you to work, the promise of extra money when you're already comfortable can actually stifle creativity. That is the conclusion of Teresa Amabile, head of the Entrepreneurial Management Unit at Harvard Business School and the only tenured professor at a top business school to devote her entire research program to the study of creativity. She and her research team collected nearly 12,000 daily journal entries from 238 people working on creative projects in seven companies in the high-tech, chemical, and consumer products industries. She discovered that people are most creative when they are self-motivated and when they care about their work. But when they start to worry about their bonuses and pay-for-performance plans, they start to get risk averse. To "guarantee results" they stick to what has worked before and they are much less likely to take risks.

When we are chasing after financial goals, we usually think we are seeking self-improvement. Yet we're actually more motivated by a *fear of loss* than the *dream of gain*. Our greatest fear is losing ground.

Economists and psychologists discovered that people expect *losing* money will have more impact than *gaining* money. Most people, for example, would refuse a bet that gives us an 85 percent chance of doubling our life savings and a 15 percent chance of losing it. The likely prospect of a big gain doesn't outweigh the more unlikely prospect of a big loss.

When people are asked whether they would prefer to have a job at which they earned $30,000 the first year, $40,000 the second year, and $50,000 the third year, or a job at which they earned $60,000 then $50,000 then $40,000, they generally prefer the job with the increasing wages, even though they will be earning less money overall. We would rather be making less than feel like we're "losing."

When you focus on something bad happening, it tends to go like this: "If I don't finish this report on time my boss is going to fire me, and I won't have enough money to pay my rent, and my wife will leave me, and she'll take the kids and marry that Todd guy with the BMW. I'll be so depressed that I'll never be able to work again. I'll get in a fight with a guy in the homeless shelter over whose sleeping bag touched whose, and I'll get kicked out and I'll end up living under a bridge in a cardboard box." That's pretty bad.

Of course, the worst case scenario hardly every happens. Even when it does, we fail to predict how resilient we'll be. We have what Daniel Gilbert, author of *Stumbling on Happiness*, calls a "psychological immune system."

When people are asked to imagine how they would feel if something terrible happened, they almost always overestimate how foul their life would be. But in the wake of tragedy, human minds get to work to reset the balance. We re-categorize those episodes as "transformative life experiences," and then get on with the business of living.

Gilbert blames our "inability to take the perspective of the person to whom the rest of our lives will happen" on the inescapable fact that we imagine the future by projecting our current selves forward. "We fail to recognize that our future selves won't see the world the way we see it now."

So if you were to end up living under a bridge, you might find that you took great pride in making the best newspaper blankets on the block, and you might be grateful that you had a refrigerator box and not a washing machine box like that loser Homeless Joe.

Studies of those who survive major traumas suggest that the vast majority do quite well, thank you very much. And a significant portion claim that their lives were enhanced by the experience.

Thus actor Christopher Reeve, after being paralyzed in a riding accident, wrote the book *Nothing Is Impossible*, and Michael J. Fox, after being diagnosed with Parkinson's disease, wrote books called *Always Looking Up* and *Lucky Man*, in which he said: "If you were to rush into the room right now and announce that you had struck a deal—with God, Allah, Buddha, Christ, Krishna, Bill Gates, whomever—in which the ten years since my diagnosis could be taken away, traded in for ten more years as the person I was before—I would, without a moment's hesitation, tell you to take a hike."

Just be careful. Too much creativity can lead to the kind of innovation that takes you out of the ranks of the poor.

"In a sense, art is always about conflict—formally and socially. It's certainly harder to appreciate the expression of conflict coming from someone who is rich and obviously doesn't have to live with conflict than it is coming from someone for whom survival is a more vital issue."

—STEVEN DURLAND, U.S. ARTIST AND WRITER

Be a (Social) Capitalist!

> "Men can do jointly what they cannot do singly; and the union of minds and hands, the concentration of their power, becomes almost omnipotent."

—DANIEL WEBSTER, AMERICAN POLITICIAN

One of my favorite films is director Ron Howard's *Apollo 13*. It is one of the only big-budget Hollywood pictures I know of that celebrates the actions of a team rather than those of a rugged individual. There are no cowboys, no rogue cops, and no Han Solo (whose name even suggests going it alone). The task of bringing the endangered Apollo 13 astronauts back to Earth fell on the shoulders of a huge team of tech geeks working with slide rules. When the stakes are high, teamwork rules the day, and contrary to American mythology, there is real drama in cooperation.

This brings me to my point. Building a rocket to send to the moon takes financial capital. Getting stranded astronauts back to the planet takes *human* capital.

There are two ways to get something done. You can be a rugged individual, in which case you'll probably have to throw a lot of money at your problem. This is usually effective and requires the least immediate effort. Or you can draw on your network of people who like you, respect you, and want to help. Both methods require a big investment beforehand. In one case, you have to work a lot of hours to build up dough. In the other, you have to put in a lot of time and attention to building friendships. Being a social capitalist is great because building up friendships is fun whether you use the capital or not, and the biggest rewards go to the nicest people.

Look at any exceptional individual. Chances are, if you look closely enough, you will see that he is exceptional because he is not an individual. He is someone who has the resources to hire a good staff. To the leader goes the credit and the impression that he achieved everything on his own. John F. Kennedy is remembered for saying, "Ask not what your country can do for you, ask what you can do for your country." When his speech writer, Ted Sorensen, was asked if he was the author of that famous line he once said, "Ask not." Oprah Winfrey has researchers and fashion consultants and makeup artists and corporate sponsors willing to fund her dream-come-true give-aways. Academic discoveries would not be possible without the work of uncredited graduate students. Business leaders have armies of workers and communications staffs to control the PR. The president has a full cabinet of experts to help him keep on top of things. Some scholars believe William Shakespeare's plays were not the work of one man, but the collective work of the William Shakespeare the-atrical company.

Even if you're broke, overdrawn, and have massive debt, you probably have more capital than you think when you figure in your social capital. Yet as valuable as social capital can be, more and more these days we are shunning clubs and community organizations; we're less likely to have friends over for dinner and less likely to know our neighbors than we were in days gone by. More of us are living alone. About 10 percent of Americans did in 2000, and the average household contained only 2.6 people. More than four times as many Americans describe themselves as lonely now than did in 1957. That leaves us running faster and faster after financial capital to bridge the gap.

A person with social capital, however, can achieve as much or more than someone with a lot of greenbacks to throw around. Ask Chris Jones. Jones is an open and affable British filmmaker who got it into his head a few years ago to make a short film worthy of an Oscar. If he was going to go for the gold, he would need a great cast, talented crew, and good equipment. He had a great script, he had vision, and he had a lot of supportive friends. He only lacked one thing. Money. So what did he do? He tried not to sing out of key. (He got by with a little help from his friends.)

"We made the lofty claim that we were going to win an Oscar, and people started to believe in the dream." he said. "I basically asked everyone I'd ever met for £50—What better way to set a goal than publicly. 'Look I'm going to try to win an Oscar, and I need your help.' At no point after that was it possible for me to go to bed when I was tired if I knew that extra thing needed to be done. There was nowhere to hide. And that created an overwhelming drive. As soon as people see that, everyone's infected by it. It's like the lunatics are out of the asylum then. We lunatics congregate together and do stupid things like make films."

Jones managed to raise £22,000 for his project, which was quite enough—as long as no one got paid. Fortunately, Jones's Oscar aspiration, feel-good script, and charisma also attracted talented artists who were willing to donate their time and energy. The film stars veteran Scottish actor Bill Patterson as Old Bill and Devon Murray (Seamus, Harry's roommate in the Harry Potter films) as Young Bill. It was the only time cinematographer Vernon Layton, whose credits include *The Englishman Who Went Up a Hill and Came Down a Mountain* and *I Still Know What You Did Last Summer*, had donated his time to a film project. Jones also managed to get friends to donate equipment and film stock.

"That was part and parcel of saying, 'We're not just going to make a short film, we're going to win an Oscar.' We need a cast now that is worthy of an Oscar, and suddenly everything was raised to that sort of level. I run a very optimistic ship, and I believe as an independent filmmaker you can't be a ruler, you have to be a leader. So I'm always picking up lights and so on so people can see I'm busting my gut along with everyone else. They know I've done enough drafts of the script to get it right; they know that I've seen every actor possible; that I hired the best DP and the best editor; and we're shooting on film and not digital. By virtue of the actual physical technology, it requires that you find people who are experienced and passionate about that aspect of the craft, which then raises the game. When people see we've pushed the boat out in that way, they want to get on board."

The result, *Gone Fishing,* is ten minutes of visually lush and emotionally touching storytelling. It has won numerous awards, received critical praise, and, yes, it was short-listed (but not nominated) for the coveted golden statue.

Ironically, had Jones offered to pay his cast and crew a token salary, he would most likely not have had very good results. Money, researchers have discovered, has a pronounced social distancing effect. We have internalized two ways of relating to other people, one is a "social norm," when you help people out because it is the right, socially cohesive thing to do; the other is the "business norm," where someone pays you to perform a task.

Following the social norm, if two people are fixing a porch together and one says to the other, "Hand me a hammer," you do not expect the other person to reply, "That's not in my job description."

The moment money enters into the equation everything changes. Numerous studies have demonstrated that people are much less willing to help out and do a little extra for someone if they see it as a business transaction. Here is just one example.

In a 2004 experiment, researchers James Heyman and Dan Ariely asked three different groups to perform a simple menial task, dragging as many circles across the computer screen as they could in five minutes. Each of the three groups was offered something different for performing this task. One group was told they were doing this as a favor to the researchers, the second was told they would get 50 cents, the third $5.

The group that performed the task as a favor dragged the most circles across the screen, more than the $5 group and significantly more than the 50-cent group. People seem to be willing to work as a volunteer, and to work for a fair wage, but when they believe they are being underpaid, performance really suffers.

You don't even need to get paid for the distancing effect to kick in. Even the slightest hint of money seems to make people more self-focused and socially isolated. Here's just how slight the hint can be:

Researcher Kathleen Vohns conducted a series of experiments on just this question. In one, she and her team invited subjects to take part in a "get acquainted" conversation. The subjects and experimenters met near a desk with a computer running a screen saver. One screen saver had fish swimming, the other was a blank screen, and the third showed a shower of money. They were not asked anything about the screen saver. It was just flashing away in the background. Even so, the people who had money in their peripheral vision put a significantly greater distance between their own chair and that of the experimenter. When they were asked if they would like to work on a task alone or with other people, 72 percent of the money-screen group chose to be alone. Only 16 percent of the other groups did the same. Researchers have had similar results by seating subjects near posters showing dollar bills and having them do word puzzles that contain financial expressions. People subtly prodded to think about money were less likely to engage in social activities and less generous when asked to make donations to charities.

It's not surprising, then, that a 1993 study found that economics students—who spend most of their time focused on money—act more selfishly than students of other disciplines. Whether the money makes them that way or they are attracted to money because they are that way is an open question.

Factoid: Americans now spend six hours a week shopping and only forty minutes playing with our kids.

Remember King Midas? Everything he touched turned to gold. Do you ever find yourself sitting in your office cubicle, wishing you had just a little bit of that touch? In our culture we use the good king as a metaphor for business success and for good luck in general. There is even an auto repair chain that wants you to "trust the Midas touch."

We all remember the story, but we've completely forgotten the moral. Having everything turn to gold was anything but good luck for poor Midas. When he tried to tend his garden, he killed the plants. He couldn't eat because his food turned into metallic chunks. His water, his bed linens, and presumably his toilet paper were converted into unusable glittering material. (If you took your car to a place with a literal Midas touch, you couldn't drive it any more.) Finally even Midas's family and friends were converted into lifeless gold statues. That is one serious demonstration of the social distancing effect of money! Midas was left despondent and alone. The moral of the Midas story? Wealth isn't all it's cracked up to be. Relationships are worth more than gold.

Edward Filene, of the Boston department store fame, was totally consumed by business. In his thirties, while he was traveling on a streetcar with his fiancée, he ran into a business acquaintance. By the end of the ride, he had concluded a deal, but lost his future bride. She had walked out on him without his even noticing it.

How to Eat:
An Overview

"I had to sell my saucepan so I could buy something to cook in it."

—WOODY GUTHRIE, AMERICAN FOLK SINGER

Here is something to keep in mind as you plan your successful life of poverty. You're still going to have to eat. Eating is fundamental. The word *job*, as a matter of fact, derives from the Middle English *jobbe*, meaning "mouthful." (Insert your own joke about the "oldest profession" here.) Our jobs are our way of getting fed.

There was a time in our not-too-distant past that our entire lives were taken up with the quest for food in the form of buffalo and wild turkeys. The authors of the book *Mean Genes* suggest that the food-based economy of our past is what keeps us in debt (not to mention fat) today. See, back in our hunter-gatherer days, our big problem was avoiding starvation. There were no refrigerators, no freezers. There was also no money, so you couldn't sell what was leftover and use the cash to buy someone else's leftover gazelle tomorrow.

If you managed to down a water buffalo, you had to figure out some way to keep it from rotting before you could make use of it. The best way to do that was to eat it and store it on your body as fat. Our lizard brains interpret our metaphorical "bread" as literal bread. We'd better eat it all up as fast as we can, or it will rot away. This explains both your expanding waistline and your diminishing bank account. Consuming as much as you can as quickly as you can is a great survival technique in a world of scarcity. In a Piggly-Wiggly world, it's a little bit crazy.

Thankfully, even with most of your reserves going to support your dependents at Bank of America, you can find ways to eat.

This is not going to be like most books on thrift and assume you can solve this problem and build up a huge savings just by cutting out your daily Starbucks, your weekly trip to the movies, and your once-a-day restaurant meal. If you're still in a position to do all these things, then you already know this. To the truly broke, the idea of a daily Starbucks and a weekly movie habit sounds like the height of luxury.

I'm not even going to talk about the "Coupon Queen" who manages to buy a whole cart of specially selected consumer items on double-coupon day for $1.98. You probably have things to do with your time other than clip coupons, drive from store to store, and plan your calendar for bargain days. It's a perfectly good hobby if you like to do it, but there are more ingenious ways to score free and cheap food.

Factoid: A *Consumerist* reader discovered that it takes 35 Taco Bell hot sauce packets to refill your store-bought hot sauce bottle.

With little to no money you can have an Epicurean feast. Of course, you have to remember one or two things about Epicurus. Epicurus was an ancient Greek philosopher whose name has become synonymous with hedonism because he advocated the pursuit of sensual pleasure, which he believed was the goal of a happy life. Relishing in sensual pleasure was controversial, of course, especially when people stopped to imagine what might be happening at a co-educational Epicurean school set up by some wealthy patrons. The appeal of a philosophy of pleasure is obvious, and schools promoting Epicurus's philosophy started to pop up all over the Mediterranean world. Epicurus's reputation was such that his name came into the language as a description for the pursuit of pleasure, and by extension to mean anything luxurious, sensual, and gluttonous.

As is often the case, however, Epicurus's reputation was spread by people who hadn't delved too deeply into his teachings. The main problem seems to be the definition of the word *pleasure*, which most people associate with abundance and overindulgence. Epicurus had an entirely different definition of the word. As Alain de Botton wrote in *Consolations of Philosophy*:

> "He had not meant to deceive. His devotion to pleasure was far greater than even the orgy accusers could have imagined. It was just that after rational analysis, he had come to some striking conclusions about what actually made life pleasurable—and fortunately for those lacking a large income, it seemed that the essential ingredients of pleasure, however elusive, were not very expensive."

His recipe for a simple life included friendship, self-sufficiency, and creative thought. Epicurus and his friends opted out of the hustle and bustle of the Athens business world and formed a self-sustaining community. They grew their own cabbage, onions, and artichokes, and in the evenings sat in the garden to reflect upon life.

"Simplicity did not affect the friends' sense of status," wrote de Botton, "because by distancing themselves from the values of Athens, they had ceased to judge themselves on a material basis. There was no need to be embarrassed by bare walls, and no benefit and showing off gold.... The crux of Epicurus's argument is that if we have money without friends, freedom, and an analysed life, we will never be truly happy. And if we have them, but are missing the fortune, we will never be unhappy."

So what did a true Epicurean feast consist of? The philosopher enjoyed a meal of vegetables, olives, and bread and drank water instead of wine. He reportedly told a friend, "Send me a pot of cheese, so that I may have a feast whenever I like."

Needless to say, a pleasurable feast is something to be savored, not to be chugged down on the go. In 2002, 25 percent of fast-food meals in America were consumed in vehicles.* Nothing says "America" more than the Golden Arches. The combination of fatty food, fast service, a complete lack of ambiance all delivered by a streamlined free market business machine—it's everything American distilled into one grinning plastic clown.

Many British people, incidentally, believe that thru *is the standard spelling of* through *in America. It is not. It only appears that way on road signs.*

That said, most U.S. meals are not eaten in a vehicle, although we do eat out quite a bit. *Restaurants USA* confirms that one in five meals (usually lunch) is prepared in a commercial setting. When we do eat at home, it often feels more rushed than in days gone by. Stovetop and microwave meals rule the day. Even kitchen design favors a hyped-up lifestyle. In old-fashioned kitchens, there was a kitchen table right in the middle where you could pull up a chair and chat as you shucked beans. Modern kitchens favor countertops and work spaces where the cook has to stand.

The moral of the story is this: the key to a feast is not the price or exotic nature of the ingredients, it is the degree to which you savor the experience. Alice Brock summed it up in *Alice's Restaurant Cookbook* this way: "It's a lovely thing—everyone sitting down together, sharing food. Breaking bread or eating together is a traditional symbol of peace. So take a moment, before you dig in, to smile at your friends."

THINGS TO BE **THANKFUL** FOR

A court decided that a Binghamton, New York, dentist could not seize and auction the false teeth of a bankrupt woman. The teeth were ruled to be "a part of a bankrupt's physical person."

Spam Ramen* Supreme

2 cups water
2 packages ramen noodles
½ cup frozen green peas
1 can Spam
½ cup sliced green onions
1 tablespoon sesame oil
garlic powder, to taste

1. Put 2 cups of water in a cooking pot and bring to a boil.
2. Once the water is boiling add your ramen noodles and peas.
3. While waiting for the noodles to become tender, cube the Spam.
4. Lightly brown the onions and Spam in sesame oil.
5. When the noodles are tender, drain and place on a plate.
6. Top noodles with browned Spam and onion mix.
7. Season with garlic powder to taste.

---

*$700 billion (the estimated price of the federal bailout of banks as of early 2009) is enough to buy 3.5 trillion (3,500,000,000,000) packs of ramen noodles. (Average price: 20 cents per pack.)

The GDP, or Is Consumption Gross?

....

"New Rule: Not everything in America has to make a profit. . . . The United States always defined capitalism, but it didn't used to define us. . . . When did the profit motive become the only reason to do anything? When did that become the new patriotism?"

—BILL MAHER, U.S. COMEDIAN

I am going to tell you two stories about a family I'll call the Stones. Adam Stone's SUV is inching along the expressway. "Why do they call it 'rush hour' if you just sit here?" he wonders ruefully. His right hand is bruised and he is angry at himself. Earlier this morning he punched a crack into his dashboard, lowering the value even more on this 147,000-mile monstrosity. He hopes the car will last another year even as he wonders how he ever became an SUV guy.

He had another fight with his wife, Andrea, this morning over who is going to take Tommy to his soccer practice and band lesson. Susie's dance class is having its portraits done at the same time. It seems as if every time they turn around there is another unexpected expense— dance class photos and costumes, new soccer cleats. Tommy's birthday is coming up and he's expecting a Playstation Portable, which means they will have to get a few games or it's useless. Andrea's hours have already been cut back at her job, and they're announcing another round of layoffs next week. Where will they find the money? Already they are late on their Discover Card payment, and they wrote a check they knew was bad so the auto insurance would get there before the deadline. The overdraft fees wiped them out for the whole month, but at least the insurance wasn't canceled. Adam is working as much overtime as he can get, but then Andrea gets frustrated at him for not being around. He just can't win.

It seems like all they do these days is fight. They even tried seeing a marriage counselor a few times, but it seemed like just another thing on a crowded to-do list. Is a divorce lawyer going to be the next call? It seems like only yesterday that Adam and Andrea moved into their dream house. It was too big for the two of them, but the family would grow into it. It was a bit more than they could afford, but the realtor assured them its value would go up and it was a great investment. They started decorating and furnishing with abandon. Adam felt like he had really made it when he looked at that house. Now he feels like he's on the verge of going under all the time.

Adam is now smoking two packs a day. As he tries to light his fourth cigarette of the morning his bruised hand shakes, the embers fall on his shirt, and as he tries to brush them off before they burn him, he crashes into the car in front of him. Suffering a concussion, he is rushed to the hospital in an ambulance while his blue SUV is towed to a repair shop.

Now let's imagine another life for the Stones. Adam and Andrea live in a modest house just outside of town. Adam has been on a health kick. He kicked the cigarette habit three years ago and has been riding his bike to work.* He has lost thirty pounds and feels great. With Adam riding his bike, the Stones can get by with only one car. The savings in gasoline and insurance payments has made it possible for Andrea to be a stay-at-home mom and to work on her painting while the kids are at school. People have told her that some of her paintings are good enough to sell, but she could never do that. When it is warm enough, Andrea and the kids work on the garden together. Andrea loves to get her hands dirty. There is something almost meditative about the repetitive task of pulling up the weeds. By late summer, the garden is bursting with tomatoes, cucumbers, and peppers. Andrea has become famous for her homemade gazpacho. All of the Stones' friends have to come over at some point in the summer to sit at the picnic table and sample it, and no one goes home without a big bag of vegetables from the garden. There are far too many for one family. With a little resourcefulness, Andrea has worked out an exchange with a neighbor. Jon used to be in a rock band in his youth, and he has been giving Tommy guitar lessons on Saturdays in exchange for some of the vegetable bounty and a little painting around his house. Andrea and Adam feel healthy, resourceful, and successful as parents.

Now, which scenario is better for our society?

If you said B, you are not an economist.

Economists and politicians measure our nation's economic health in terms of our Gross Domestic Product (GDP) or Gross National Product (GNP). Simply put, the GDP is the monetary value of all the goods

---

*"Ultimate Cheapskate" Jeff Yeager argues that the bicycle is the fastest machine ever invented when you factor in the time it takes to earn enough money to buy a car and pay for insurance and gasoline compared with the cost to get a bike on the road.

and services bought and sold in the economy. The GNP is the monetary value of all the goods and services bought and sold by U.S. nationals, whether in the country or abroad.

The GDP/GNP are like Seth Green in those Rally's ads from the early 1990s. Every time you spend money, the GDP goes up. *Cha-ching!* It doesn't matter if you spend it on a Playstation Portable—*Cha-ching!* Or chain smoking—*Ching*! Or divorce layers—*Ching*! Or having your car towed—*Ching*! Or hospital bills—*Ba-dah-bing*! If Adam had gotten lung cancer and needed chemotherapy it would really improve the GDP. *Cha-ching*!

> **Factoid:** In the world economy, weapons and drugs are the number one and number two industries.

Staying away from the gas pump, building up savings, going to church, doing volunteer work, creating art, and growing vegetables that you give away do nothing at all to spur "economic growth" as economists understand it. If you take care of your children at home, the economy stagnates. If you send your kids off to a babysitter and money changes hands—voilà! Growth! Sit in the shade of a beautiful tree and the GDP ticks down. Cut down the shade trees, put up a parking lot, and buy a big air conditioner to keep things cool, and now we're making real economic progress. Have an insanely long commute that increases your stress and robs you of time with your kids? Hey, you're buying more gasoline; you're paying more to the babysitter. Cool!

More economic growth. Trash disposal costing our country $50 billion? Hey, we spent $50 billion. Great news! Guess what? Divorce lawyers are costing us $60 billion a year.

The GDP is the ultimate zen master and lives entirely in the now. Natural resources, research, and development are *not capital* to the GDP. Education, health care, and social services are valuable only to the extent that someone makes cash from them *today*. That makes schooling a fairly wasteful endeavor from an economic point of view.

Where a normal person might see the clear-cutting of a forest or the draining of an oil reserve as the liquidation of an asset, GDP counts this depletion as current income. It's all good. This is a bit like burning your house down and counting it as progress that you had to build a new one.

The GDP: We sold another thing today!

Sane Person: What was the thing?

The GDP: Does it matter?

Sane Person: What do you do with it? Is it useful? Is it decorative; something?

The GDP: Huh? What kind of question is that? We sold a thing.

Sane Person: But did we lose anything by producing it?

The GDP: It's not my job to measure that. Did I mention we sold a thing?

Sane Person: Do we need this thing?

The GDP: Of course we do—it's growth. We're growing.

Sane Person: What are we growing toward? What is our growth for?

The GDP: What are you, a communist?

This aspect of the GDP led Canadian economist Mark Anielski to quip, ". . . everything that costs a buck gets added to the gross domestic product, but nothing is ever subtracted. How clever—I wish I could do that with my check book. . . . It's as if you were doing your finances with only the addition key on the calculator functioning—nothing is ever subtracted. How can this be? Nothing is a cost; everything goes in the plus column? How did this evolve? What were they smoking? And more importantly, how do we get off this crazy thing?"

If we're not measuring our nation's health in terms of GDP or GNP we usually rely on the Consumer Confidence Index, which measures "consumers' expectations" toward conditions that will influence their eagerness to go to the mall.

Could it be that "growth" and "progress" are overrated?

You may have had an inkling, a sinking feeling that something wasn't quite right in our shining economy. During those boom years in the 1980s and '90s, all the reports on the nightly news were telling you that the economy was going great. We had a GDP that rivaled any on Earth. If things were so great, why didn't you feel like you were doing that well? You probably assumed the problem was you, that you were the one who was crazy or the one who was failing to live up to your potential. Well guess what? You were not crazy at all, and you weren't the only one who failed to thrive as the GDP rose.

Scholars have developed a number of alternative ways to measure our nation's health. The U.S. Quality of Life index, a system invented by scholars to quantify not only production and income but such variables as health, leisure time, and living conditions, has been falling since the 1970s. Redefining Progress, creators of the Genuine Progress Indicator, which values volunteerism and accounts for the loss of leisure from excess hours at work and the loss of natural capital, has likewise measured a continuous drop in well-being since 1970.

"The reason markets in advanced economies fail to do much to promote, let alone maximize, well being," wrote professor Robert E. Lane in *Loss of Happiness in Market Democracies*, "is that the things that contribute most to well-being, especially companionship and family life, are market externalities."

"Market externalities"—isn't that a great phrase to describe your relationship with your children, being in love, and the sense of wonder and awe when sitting near a waterfall?

Perhaps it is time to take stock of your own life and measure quality in your own terms. John Ivanko and Lisa Kivirist, a pair of downshifters who write on green and sustainability issues, decided to start basing their choices on an ecologically modeled Diversified Quality of Life Index, which measures such things as the health of relationships, enjoyment of work, level of satisfaction with life, and opportunities for community involvement. When they measured their jobs by these standards they found that "much of our income-producing work does not command high compensation." Does yours?

The Lottery Is Not an Investment Strategy, but It Is Fun

When you get to the end of your financial tether, it sometimes seems that the only way you'll ever dig out is by winning the lottery. Of course your odds of winning are only slightly higher than the odds of your getting a jet pack and flying to the moon.

One of the great things about being broke, however, is how much more joy you can get from the lottery, bingo, and sweepstakes. Thinking about what you will buy with your raffle or contest winnings is a moment to imagine a life free from financial stress and worry. The amount of pleasure it brings you is directly proportionate to the amount of budget stress you have. By this measure, a broke person gets so much more bang for the buck. Forget about winning, and focus on this prize.

Sweepstakes entries cost nothing but the time to fill them out, and they offer the same fantasy-to-debt ratio as expensive lottery tickets and even more expensive casino gambling. If you must buy lottery tickets, never buy more than one at a time.* Remember, you're buying a moment of relief. With one ticket, you have one opportunity to imagine what you'll do when you've paid off your debt. If you buy five tickets, your odds of winning don't go up that much, and you're still only getting one chance to imagine being rich.

---

*I am grateful to the originator of the single lottery ticket theory, Kim Tunnicliff who was the director of the Ford Institute for Public Service at Albion College

A note of caution. If you find that you enjoy the lottery and Bingo, watch yourself, or you might move on to higher-stakes forms of gambling, such as the stock market. No self-respecting broke person does that, although quite a few of the nouveau broke got there because they did so in the past.

Remember: as with all things relating to money, the acquiring is much more pleasing than the having. Winning the lottery feels great. Having won the lottery is just another thing you get used to.

The tales of woe among lottery winners are too many to mention here. In one study, Roy Kaplan of the Florida Institute of Technology tracked one thousand lottery winners over a span of ten years. Most had no idea what to do with the money. A surprising number reported that they were less happy six months later because they left jobs that had been a source of self-esteem and gained money they had done nothing to earn. In fact, a few years ago the *New York Times* ran a story on the Millionaire Circle Club, a support group for past lottery winners.

7

Autonomy vs. Independence: Further Reflections on Social Capital

....

"Study the system which you see all around you, of material, animal and rational existence, in its minutest, or in it grandest portions. Nothing you see is insulated; nothing existing for itself alone. Every part of creation bears perpetually on some other part, and they must subsist together. Indeed, the whole universe, as far as we have penetrated it, seems to be a mighty and complex system of mutual subserviency."

**—JOSEPH STEVENS BUCKMINSTER
(1784-1812), U.S. MINISTER**

When Europeans first arrived in North America, they discovered a vast open wilderness. It was virgin territory, just waiting to be explored. Virgin territory, that is, with the exception of the diverse communities that were inconveniently already located there. The Europeans determined that the Natives were "uncivilized"—they didn't even have guns! Although the label said more about the Europeans than it did the Native Americans, it had enormous staying power.

What does it take for a culture to be "civilized"? Great works of art, perhaps? Advanced agriculture? Well-developed religious and social beliefs? The Native Americans had all of those. So what was so "uncivilized" about them?

When we use the word *civilized* in general speech, we usually mean "refined and enlightened." We think of porcelain teacups and opera. When anthropologists speak of a "civilized" society, they generally mean "having a complex division of labor." The further away you get from the earth and a relationship with nature—the more you rely on financial rather than social capital—the more "civilized" you become.

What you may not know is that many European settlers thought the Natives had it right. Tired of the rat race of "civilization" as they knew it, they tried to defect. Historian Gary Nash noted that "facilitated by the fact that some Indians lived among the English as day laborers, while a number of settlers fled to Indian villages rather than endure the rigors of life among the autocratic English."

In his *Letters from an American Farmer*, Michel Guillaume Jean de Crevecour, (taking a deep sigh and pausing after scratching out that name with a quill) wrote: "There must be in the Indians' social bond something singularly captivating, and far superior to be boasted of among us; for thousands of Europeans are Indians, and we have no examples of even one of those Aborigines having from choice become Europeans."

Hernando De Soto had to post guards to keep his people from fleeing to Indian villages. The Pilgrims imposed extreme punishments, up to the death penalty, if any of their ranks were caught running away to join the Natives. The Pilgrims also had to forbid men from copying the local style. They made it illegal for men to wear long hair. Damn hippies!

Even Benjamin Franklin, the guy on the $100 bill, said, "No European who has tasted Savage Life can afterwards bear to live in our societies."

All About the Benjamins

From the "Do as I Say, Not as I Do" file: Ben Franklin, who coined the motto "a penny saved is a penny earned," saved his pennies at Philadelphia's Bank of America. In 1940, auditors looked at all the bank's records going back to its first accounts and found that Franklin was overdrawn on his account at least three times each week.

The fairly unconventional definition of "savage" as "irresistible" begs the question: What was it about native life that was so appealing that the Europeans felt they had to enact laws to maintain their social hold?

Anthropologist Frederick Turner contrasted the Native American belief that we are "part of the total living universe [where] spiritual health is to be had only by accepting this condition and by attempting to live in accordance with it" with a Eurocentric worldview that he called "a shockingly dead view of creation. We ourselves are the only things in the universe to which we grant an authentic vitality, and because of this we are not fully alive."

Is it possible that our Hollywood westerns got their cowboys-and-Indians narrative wrong, and that as early as the 1600s, Westerners were already beginning to feel a sense of loss in their detachment from the natural world and the other people in it?

We've talked about the Indians—let's talk about that cowboy. The Lone Ranger is as much a myth as the Savage Indian, of course. Real frontier folk were surely rugged, for they had to survive in an unfamiliar environment. But they were not going it alone. They relied on their social capital, their wagon trains, and relationships with the members of the Native nations who frequently traded with them and guided them through the terrain, acting as interpreters.

The story of the solo cowboy, riding into the sunset singing "Don't Fence Me In," didn't start to evolve until after the Civil War. Jennifer Moskowitz of the University of South Dakota explained in *Americana: The Journal of American Popular Culture*, "America after the Civil War was in a state of national upheaval and in desperate need of a . . . unifying, nationalist icon to move it beyond the ravages of the Civil War and the Englishness of Southern agrarian society into industrialism and capitalism. . . . Into the West rode the American cowboy, whose mythic figure and setting were equally significant and carefully shaped by authors, artists, and political figures."

He may have been largely a fiction, but the cowboy riding off into the vast wilderness with nothing but his horse, wits, and a Smith & Wesson continues to shape our thinking. A real American makes it on his own, or he doesn't make it at all. This view makes us all a little bit poor when it comes to social capital.

Australian professor Richard Eckerdsley has spent many years studying what gives people a sense of well-being. He is, in essence, a scholar of what makes life worth living. Eckerdsley makes a distinction between *autonomy* (the ability to act according to our internalized values and beliefs) and *independence* (not being reliant on or influenced by others).

In everyday conversation, the opposite of *independence* is *dependence*. Who wants to think of herself as "dependent"? Babies are dependent. We love them in spite of, or maybe because of, their helplessness. Yet we're in a pretty big hurry to get them out of diapers and teach them to wipe their own noses. We spend most of their childhoods asking what they're going to be when they grow up. (Some people have argued that we do this because we're looking for ideas.)

We grown-ups don't want to be seen as a bunch of helpless crybabies. The result is that most of the time, we find it less onerous to pay someone to perform a task than to cash in our social capital. But when we do this we're throwing that dependent baby out with the bath water. If you don't depend on others you need more money, which means you'll have to work more hours, which means you have less time to devote to relationships. Which means you need more money, which means . . .

Has it seemed to you that in the past couple of decades the term "responsibility" has shifted from meaning "responsibility to others" to meaning "you take care of yours and I'll take care of mine"?

This stems from confusion between autonomy and independence. "Or, to put it somewhat differently," wrote Eckerdsley, "'thinking *for* ourselves' has been redefined as 'thinking *of* ourselves.'"

Ironically, when you are focused entirely on independence, you may end up sacrificing your autonomy. One of the best ways to take care of yourself as a responsible grown-up is by making an *autonomous* choice not to act *independently*.

That is what author and world hunger activist Lynne Twist discovered when she observed members of the Amazonian Achuar, a culture that does not use money at all. (Pause for a brief moment here and imagine a world where money doesn't exist.)

"When the Achuar are in their rain forest home they are prosperous and have everything they need, and have been for centuries, even millennia," Twist wrote. "One step out of the rain forest into our world and they can't eat, find shelter, or live for any length of time without money. Money is not an option; it is a requirement." Seeing how much more *autonomous* people could be living in harmony in a money-free world led Twist to reconsider her own relationship with the green. She eventually founded the Soul of Money institute (www.soulofmoney.org) to mentor others and help them "move from an economy of fear, consumption, and scarcity, to an economy of sufficiency, sustainability, and generosity." Maybe it's time for you and your complexes about money to spend a little time apart as well.

———◆———

"Abolish luxury if you please, but leave the soil, upon which alone all the virtues and all that is precious in the human character grow; poverty—honest poverty."

—ANDREW CARNEGIE, U.S. INDUSTRIALIST

Bohemian Rhapsody: Define Yourself as an Artist

....

"There are moments in which art almost obtains the dignity of manual labor."

—OSCAR WILDE, IRISH PLAYWRIGHT

People assume "starving" and "artist" go together, and you can wear it as a badge of honor as you tilt your beret. Van Gogh sold only one painting in his lifetime. Dickens was nearly bankrupted. Percy and Mary Shelly spent much of their life moving around Europe to escape creditors. *Don Quixote* was written in Cervantes's declining years in a desperate attempt to make some money he could leave to his debt-ridden family. William Shakespeare never earned more than an annual income of £20 (£3,313 in today's money) in his life. If these great artists had it so bad, then clearly artists need to be measured by a different yard stick.

And you know what? Starving artists make better lovers. It's true! At least according to a recent *Redbook* magazine survey. They asked their female readers "who makes the best husband by profession." The winners were artists followed by truck drivers and mechanics. The worst? Doctors. Artists got a 100 percent score for "taking their time" at foreplay.

The right temporal lobe of the brain is responsible for orgasms. It is also the section associated with artistic creativity and religious ecstasy. A recent study of 425 British men and women found that "creative types" had more sex partners. They averaged between four and ten while the "less creative" typically had three. The researchers concluded that the more creative the study participants were, the more partners they had. (Unfortunately, my source failed to mention the name of the study or explain how they determined who was "more creative.")

One of the great titles in the self-help genre is the 1989 *Do What You Love, The Money Will Follow*. It promises an almost mystical connection between right livelihood and wealth. Follow your heart, and riches will come to you. Defer immediate security for a grand payoff down the line. It is a book that encourages you to take risks.

I agree with the first part of this title. Do what you love: Seek out your right livelihood. Most people find themselves fighting for a place in a system that was created by someone else. Why should you be resigned to that when you can make your own way in the world? But I would have to amend the title to say you should do what you love whether the money follows or not. (Is this why I am not a best-selling author?)

Expect buckets of money, and you're sure to be disappointed when they fail to come quickly enough or abundantly enough. Harness your dreams to make money and you're looking at things completely backward and inside out. If your goal is to have enough money to accomplish your dreams, then you're probably on the right track.

In 2009, the Academy Award for Best Documentary went to a film called *Man on Wire*. It tells the story of Phillippe Petit, a quixotic sprite who had a dream of doing a tightrope walk between the twin towers of the World Trade Center. The French aerialist was the embodiment of the Tarot card "The Fool," unconcerned with society's conventions and confident enough to walk on air over the edge of a cliff.

Phillippe Petit had a drive to do something amazing and unconventional, to test his limits, to shock and surprise and provoke people to imagine new horizons of what can be done. But there were no practical reasons for his walk, and few practical outcomes.

Why do it? There is no reason why—no *practical* reason why. Yet the impractical things, the artistic things, need to be done. We need to have artists around to remind us that we should walk the tightrope.

It is easy for a creative type—and aren't we all creative types, really?—to become depressed when dealing with the grounded world of bank balances and credit scores. You may find that you are haunted by the label of being irresponsible.

Walking a tightrope between the World Trade Center towers took years of preparation and planning and involved hundreds of practical details. It required money to fly from France to the United States several times to see the actual towers and make realistic preparations. How do impractical people move mountains and take care of all the tasks to achieve their visions?

Here is the answer: Impractical people can not. Successful creatives are *practical people*. They are detail oriented, focused, and persistent. Their focus is simply different. Did the world need to see someone walk a tightrope across the Twin Towers in order to function? Certainly not. Yet Petit decided it did. Was it practical for him to channel his energy and resources into a quixotic venture rather than the more conventional values of home, property, and so on? If he wanted to achieve his vision, absolutely.

Spending money on a plane ticket to America to scope out the Twin Towers was a much more practical choice for Petit, whose goal was that high-wire walk, than spending money on a nice house would be.

The great strength of money, the very reason for its existence, is also its greatest weakness. In the days of the barter system, a farmer traded a cow for a chair. The problem was, the guy who had the chair had to want a cow and the guy with the cow had to want a chair. It's not a big problem if you're one of the people who grows food. It's harder if you're the person who makes, say, egg timers.

You wouldn't want to trade a whole cow for one egg timer. A cow has to be worth at least fifty egg timers. The problem is the farmer now has forty-nine egg timers that he doesn't need, and doesn't know what to do with. He can trade them to someone else, of course, but he needs to find someone who happens to want a box of egg timers and to have something the farmer wants in return.

So we came up with a system whereby pieces of metal or paper symbolize units of value. In America we use green pieces of paper because, as everyone knows, green is the color of money.

With the invention of money, the egg timer maker could sell 50 egg timers to 50 different people and collect enough units for a cow. Or he could use the paper to reimburse others for labor: "Will Work for Money."

Money was an absolutely tremendous invention that allowed us to more easily get what we need. As a universal exchange medium for services and goods it serves a great purpose. It doesn't do nearly as well as a measure of abstract things like progress, satisfaction, or creativity. Yet because we think of money as a measurement of *value*, we find it hard to imagine that anything that is not lucrative could have any value at all.

Artists are people who see the value in the things dollars can not measure. Define yourself as an artist and you give yourself permission to be "starving." This can be a great liberation.

Security is not something that comes from the outside world. The word *security* comes from the Latin *securus*, which means "without care." It is an internal state. What makes a person most secure is knowing that he is progressing toward a greater goal, whatever that may be.

Whether what you value is traditionally "artsy," like opening a photography studio, or more down to earth, like leaving the corporate rat race to spend more time with your kids, the most practical thing to do with your resources is to put them toward what makes your life worth living. Lynne Twist, a global activist and fundraiser for world hunger issues, refers to this as using money in a way that "*expresses* value rather than *determines* value."

If people say you are being impractical, what they are really saying is that they do not share your values; they do not understand your priorities. As long as you are not draining anyone else's accounts, and your basic needs are met, you should not get too hung up on what anyone else feels is practical.

Artists gain satisfaction not from idleness, but from work. The term *flow* has been applied to the creative state in which work gives you a bit of a high. The authors of *Mean Genes* wrote:

> "People experience flow when they are in control of their environment and using their skills to achieve a challenging and clear goal . . . people are more likely to experience flow while working than during leisure time. Oddly, even when experiencing flow at work, people imagine they would be happier if they were not working. So we think we'd prefer sipping gigantic beverages, yet we're happier progressing skillfully toward achievable goals."

We chronically misuse the term *creativity* as though it were a synonym for *originality* or *imagination*. The misuse of the term "creativity" makes a lot of imaginative people unhappy. They do something original, label it "creative," and feel that they should be admired and rewarded. This is like putting sugar, eggs, milk, and flour in a bowl and expecting everyone to compliment you on your delicious cake.

If you go to the section on "writing" in the book store you are likely to see an abundance of two kinds of manuals: books that aim to inspire you to get past your writer's block (these are generally labeled as books on "creativity") and guides to publishing markets. Many aspiring writers jump from *The Artist's Way* to *Writer's Market* without the intervening step of actually writing a book and then expect publishers to start having a bidding war over their journal entries.

What you don't see are many books on the very un-sexy process of sitting down, crafting, and re-crafting those original concepts until they are a viable finished product. Creativity is much more fun when you don't have to deal with the whole pesky creation part before reaping your rewards. This is a disservice in two ways. It gives people unrealistic expectations about material success, and it devalues what artists actually do by equating it with simple daydreaming. (Not that I have anything against daydreaming, but we'll get to that in a later chapter.)

Successful artists are people who *follow through* on their great ideas without any guarantees. They do what they love, whether the money follows or not. They channel all their resources—mental, emotional, and financial—into a larger creative vision.

For Philippe Petit, juggling balls, unicycles, and wire are the only practical things in which he could possibly invest. They are the only things that would make progress towards his goal. It is only when he is above the clouds that Petit is in flow. Thus walking on a wire, paradoxically, is his only true security.

By the way, it is possible that the smarter you are, the less you are interested in money. Mensa, the organization of people with genius level IQs, did a survey of its members and discovered that they rank only at median levels when it comes to financial well-being. In an interview with *Money* magazine, the executive director of Mensa explained it thusly: "They could probably make more, but they tend to do what they like, not what pays best."

So don't count yourself as a lazy bum. Consider yourself an artist of life. One note of caution. Just because Dickens was broke and you're broke doesn't make you Dickens. History may not judge it a tragedy that your talent went unrewarded. Enjoy your creativity, but be humble.

"The best way a writer can find to keep himself going is to live off his (or her) spouse. The trouble is that, psychologically at least, it's hard. Our culture teaches none of its false lessons more carefully than that one should never be dependent. Hence the novice or still unsuccessful writer, who has enough trouble believing in himself, has the added burden of shame. It's hard to be a good writer and a guilty person; a lack of self-respect creeps into one's prose."

—JOHN GARDNER, U.S. NOVELIST

Gold: The Feces of Hell!

....

"If an American meets a millionaire, his first thought is,
'What a clever man he must be!' The first thought of a
Russian is sure to be, 'How has this crook managed to grab
so much?'"

—**VLADIMIR ZHELVIS, *THE XENOPHOBE'S***
GUIDE TO THE RUSSIANS

If your life experience has led you to believe that people who hoard money are assholes, you will be pleased to know that there is at least one scientist who might back you up. Sigmund Freud, the father of psychoanalysis, made the bold connection between money and defecation in his essay "Character and Anal Eroticism." (And you thought I would write this whole book without a single mention of anal eroticism.)

If you're a covetous miser, according to Freud, you are probably an anal neurotic. Have you ever stopped to ponder why we refer to the wealthy as "filthy rich?" Something must be getting their hands dirty.

According to Freud, money is, well . . . excrement. In the mythology and fairy tales of ancient times, money is always "brought into the most intimate relationship with dirt."

There's something to that. Money is dirty and icky, and you wouldn't want it anyway. Made from organic material, it travels around the country and throughout the world passing from hand to hand, pocket to pocket. It is never washed. The average note circulates for eighteen months before it is retired.

A team of researchers from the Medical Center of the Wright-Patterson Air Force Base in Ohio counted bacteria living on sixty-eight one-dollar bills collected from people at a grocery store and a high school sporting event. They incubated each bill in a nutrient broth and grew any bacteria in a culture dish. Most of the money, 87 percent of it, contained bacteria. Most of the bacteria was not of a particularly dangerous variety, but there were also germs that could cause urinary tract infections, sore throats, food poisoning, and scariest of all, Klebsiella pneumonia and Staphylococcus aureus.

Another study conducted for the U.S. Ninth Circuit Court of Appeals concluded that more than three-quarters of the currency in circulation in Los Angeles is tainted with drug residue.

Coins are an attractive menace to little children who like to examine small shiny things by taste. More than three thousand instances of children ingesting coins were reported to U.S. poison centers in 1996. Another 21,000 children ended up in U.S. emergency rooms after swallowing coins. Hospitals report that coins are the most frequently ingested foreign objects by children. In the U.K., where they do not separate paper and metal money in their injury stats, the Royal Society for the Prevention of Accidents estimates that about 10,206 people a year are injured by some form of money.

St. Francis of Assisi, who took his vow of poverty quite literally, warned his followers to, in the words of church historian Ray Petry, "Fly from money as from the Devil himself; they were to regard it as they would excrement. A brother who so much as touched money was forced to remove it with his mouth and to put it on the dung heap outside." (Which leads one to wonder if they usually transported excrement in their mouths. Note to self: never kiss a Franciscan.)

Freud noted that in mythology "the gold which the devil gives his paramours turns into excrement after his departure, and the devil is certainly nothing else than the personification of the repressed unconscious instinctual life." He goes on to relate a superstition that links the finding of treasure with taking a dump, and he notes that the ancient Babylonians believed that gold was "the feces of hell."

Thus, Freud concludes a child who is fascinated with his bowels and what comes out of them will transform his early erotic interest into a substitute fetish for dirty money. Following Freud's lead, psychoanalyst Karl Abraham proposed that female shopaholics are also expressing a transference of forbidden dirty desires: "A compromise between instinct and repression is made by which the patient, in a spirit of defiance, does expend—not sexual libido, but an anal currency."

The forbidden lust she is playing out, Abraham argues, is specifically sado-masochistic. She lords her power over unsuspecting clerks by throwing her metaphorical scat in their faces and making them grovel for it: "Thank you for shopping . . ." and then later must punish herself when the Visa bill shows up in the mailbox. And you thought a purse was just a purse . . .

An Embarrassment of Riches

Is your teenager absolutely mortified by the idea of wearing a second-hand sweater to school? Don't give it too much thought. Your teenager would be mortified no matter what you gave him. He's a teenager. Adam Hochschild, in *Half the Way Home: A Memoir of Father and Son,* describes his humiliation at being dropped off to school in a long, black chauffered limousine when his buddies were riding bikes to school. Adam complained about it to his father, who replied, "Well, Adam, I just don't think having a car like this is anything to be ashamed of."

Think You're the Only Poor Slob in the Richest Nation on Earth?

"If you make it to the age of 35 and your job still requires a name tag, you've obviously made a serious vocational error somewhere along the line."

—DENNIS MILLER, U.S. COMEDIAN

The American Dream of social mobility has released us from some of the excessive and oppressive chains of stratified societies. It holds this truth to be self-evident: that all people are created equal. The American Dream is an engine that seeks to break down class barriers and reward individuals on their merit, not an accident of birth.

Yet our sense of what makes our nation exceptional has shifted over the centuries, argues Godfrey Hodgson in *The Myth of American Exceptionalism*. Where once we took the most pride in our social equality and class mobility, we now emphasize our exceptionalism through other values, for example "freedom." (A quality a bit more difficult to quantify.) We may still revere the concept that we are the one great classless society, but it is far from the truth, and it has become less true year after year.*

Forces such as the high cost of higher education—far higher than in any comparable developed country—make it especially challenging for a person raised in poverty in the U.S. to move up the social ladder. When economists measured class mobility between 1986 and 1991 they discovered that in comparison with European countries, Americans actually enjoyed slightly less mobility, not more.

Here's something you may not know. And shhh—don't tell your fellow Americans—when it comes to wealth in general, we are not number one. Comparison of the gross national income based on purchasing-power-parity per capita puts the U.S. ($41,557) only *third* in terms of worldwide wealth behind Luxembourg ($66, 821) and Norway ($41,941). At the bottom of that list was Timor-Leste, with a GNI of $400. (Note to Americans: Yes, it is a real country. I promise.)

But still, third in the world? Pretty good. In the land of plenty, anything you can imagine is available in an instant if you have enough credit left on your Visa Gold Card. Consider this factoid: Number of millionaires in America, out of 7.7 millionaires worldwide: 2.27 million. Now try to tell us we're not rich!

Yes, we're pretty darned good at producing millionaires. But here's the thing: we're a nation of millionaires in the same way that

---

*From a historical standpoint 1835 was the golden birth year for poor boys who aspired to strike it rich in America. The nation was still under populated with a great ratio of men to resources. Children born in 1835 came of age after the Civil War at the dawn of the industrial revolution. Historians mark this period as the greatest era of social mobility in the U.S. It is no coincidence that the ideal of the self-made man entered our culture around this time as well.

Stacey King, a rookie NBA basketball player with the Chicago Bulls, scored a victory for his team. In one of his first games with the Bulls, Michael Jordan scored 69 points and King scored 1. After the game, a reporter asked King for his reaction to the Bulls' victory, and he said: "I'll always remember this as the night Michael and I combined for 70 points."

Bill Gates is American, but that doesn't mean most Americans are Bill Gates. Gates' net worth, $46.5 billion, is more than the gross domestic product of 132 of the world's nations. (On the list of the World Bank's rankings of GDP, Gates falls between Ukraine and Morrocco.) He could literally afford to buy the world a Coke. In fact, he could buy each person in the world a twelve-pack and have change to spare. His fortune divides out to $7.50 for each person in the world. So when you take his net worth and average it with yours, you're collectively quite comfortable. But I wouldn't use that as justification to go out on a spending binge.

———◆———

"The appearance of millionaires in any society is no proof of its affluence; they can be produced by very poor countries. . . . It is not efficiency of production that makes millionaires; it is the uneven distribution of what is produced."

—JULIUS K. NYERERE (1922–1999), TANZANIAN PRESIDENT

———◆———

If the United States ever was a "classless nation" (not lacking in taste, but in social hierarchy) it is certainly not now. In 1980 the United

States was thirteenth among twenty-two leading industrial nations in income equality. Today it is *dead last*.

This point bears backing up with some facts and figures: In 1980, the average American CEO made 45 times what his employees made. By 2003, he was making 254 times what his workers made. He now makes more than *400 times* what his average employee makes.

From the late 1970s through the late 1990s, the top 1 percent of U.S. households saw their incomes increase by 157 percent. On average, these household scored after-tax income gains of nearly half a million dollars. This time period is generally described as one of the greatest economic booms in history.

For the people on the bottom, however, the boom was nothing more than a scattering of shrapnel. During this time, their net worth fell 76 percent in real dollars. (By "them" I mean the bottom 40 percent and by "during this time" I'm specifically citing figures from 1983–1998.) Entry level wages (between 1979 and 2001) for workers with a high school diploma fell by 14 percent.

So what kind of salaries are we really averaging with Mr. Gates to produce a wealthy overall nation? Nearly 30 million American workers—almost a quarter of all working people—earn less than $19,000 a year.

Factoid: If the $5.15 an hour minimum wage had risen at the same rate as CEO compensation from 1990, fast food clerks would now make $23.03 an hour.

John Cassidy explained this state of affairs in *The New Yorker*: "In the end, the argument comes down to a matter of elementary economics," he wrote. "When a working stiff demands a pay raise, it causes inflation and threatens the nation's prosperity. When a CEO gets a raise ten thousand times as large, it rewards enterprise and assures all our futures. The two phenomena, obviously, are entirely separate. Only a fool or a journalist could confuse them.

This is a big change from the Greatest Generation's day. After World War II and continuing through 1972, workers' wages increased about as fast as productivity did. A rising tide raised all boats, and we still expect that this should be the case. But after 1972, the bond between greater productivity and higher wages seems to have been broken.

Yet even if they are on the wrong side of an economic boom, most Americans don't mind too much, because they plan to move up the social ladder. The downside of the American Dream—the belief that if you work hard enough you can always make it—is that if you are not making it, you only have yourself to blame.

Americans don't complain too much when a corporate executive draws a salary larger than the GNP of most nations on earth because they secretly believe that one day, if they work hard enough, they'll be part of that elite group. Pseudo-politician "Joe the Plumber" is typical of this American attitude. He supports an economic policy that places a greater tax burden on his actual $45,000 income, in favor of cutting taxes for his hypothetical future $250,000 income.

If real wages have been falling, how have families managed to keep up? There are a few ways. We're working harder: Americans take less vacation time than their European counterparts. Between 1979 and

2000, the amount of time spent at work by the average employee increased by 162 hours—an extra month a year.

More of us are working: The single wage-earner family is becoming a relic of a bygone era. Between 1972 and 1992 the percentage of "traditional families" with Dad working and Mom at home with the kids fell from 23 percent of all U.S. families to 9 percent. By 1992, 57 percent of all families had two or more wage earners, while three out of four married-couple families with children at home had both parents working.

We're moonlighting and working part-time jobs. That's where you get the real financial rewards. For every hour a part-timer works, she makes only 62 cents for every dollar a full-time worker gets. Plus, we're sleeping less. According to some estimates, we get two hours fewer ZZZs than back in the 1960s. In one survey, four in ten adults reported sleeping less than six hours per night.

And of course there is plastic. More and more Americans have been relying on credit cards to bridge the gap between their expectations of what a middle class salary *should* buy and their *actual* purchasing power. Even if we're not destined to be Warren Buffet rich, we'll certainly be making more than we are now, so why not charge a new big-screen TV on that Master Card? Americans now owe 99 cents for each dollar they earn.

Equality Under the Law

In 1843, a British justice named Lord Maul was sentencing an itinerant beggar for bigamy. The beggar had caught his bride in the arms of another man, walked out, and later remarried without the intervening step of getting a legal divorce. As he passed his sentence, Lord Maul told the beggar what he should have done:

> You should have instructed your attorney to bring an action against the seducer of your wife for damages; that would have cost you about £100. Having proceeded thus far, you should have employed a proctor and instituted a suit in the Ecclesiastical Courts for a divorce a *mensa et thoro*: that would have cost you £200 or £300 more. When you had obtained a divorce *a mensa et throro* you had only to obtain a private act for divorce *a vinculo matrimonii*. The bill might possibly have been opposed in all its stages in both Houses of Parliament and altogether these proceedings would cost you £1,000. You will probably tell me that you never had a tenth of that sum, but that makes no difference. Sitting here as an English judge it is my duty to tell you that this is not a country where there is one law for the rich and another for the poor.

Shrinkage—or, Where Have All The Dollars Gone?

"Lavish spending can be disastrous. Don't buy any lavishes for a while."

—JIM CRITCHFIELD AND JERRY HOPKINS,
YOU WERE BORN ON A ROTTEN DAY

If you aspire to be broke, there is even more good news. Not only are your real wages likely to be lower than previous generations, your dollars aren't going as far as they used to either. Interest on your debt, hidden fees on everything from your cell phone to your airline ticket purchases, and even shrinking grocery packaging are working with you to make you the best broke person you can be!

By far, our biggest debt comes in the form of home mortgages. Research published in 1997 by the principal U.S. federal lending organization showed that $4.2 trillion was outstanding on mortgages in the U.S., a figure that had doubled in a decade, while average household incomes had risen by only a third. While the proportion of home ownership rose slightly, the total equity of U.S. housing *under mortgage* rose from 36 percent to 48 percent. What is more, the length of time it is taking the average mortgage holder to pay it off is now five years longer than a generation ago, and the amount of household income devoted to the mortgage has risen.

In other words, more people are calling themselves home owners, but far fewer of them have actually paid off the house. Many of those "home owners" were shocked this past year to discover they were not really home owners at all.

Michael Rowbotham, in *The Grip of Death*, notes that all these earning statistics involve household, not individual, income and that the figures would be even more staggering if you were to figure in how many more households now have two wage earners instead of one. "If the cost of home-buying is related to the average wage, the comparison is frightening and goes a long way to explaining why the wealthiest nation in the world cannot stop earning for a second."

Have you ever noticed that most of your credit card bills have South Dakota return addresses? It's not because bankers can't get enough of Mt. Rushmore. We used to have something in this country called usury laws. In fact we still do, they're just not worth the paper they're printed on anymore. Usury, as it is defined today is the lending of money at exorbitant interest. Back in the day each state had its own laws prohibiting the practice. In Maryland, for example, the default rate of interest is 6 percent. If you live in Maryland, however, there's a good chance you have a credit card charging you 20 percent interest or more. Go to a payday loan place in Baltimore and you can obtain a loan with an interest rate of only 300 percent.

This is because of a 1978 Supreme Court ruling *Marquette National Bank v. First of Omaha Corp*. Prior to this decision, it was assumed that even a national bank could only charge the rate of interest allowed in its customers' state. After *Marquette*, all that changed. It set the precedent that regardless of where the customers live, the bank can base its interest rates on the state in which the bank maintains its headquarters. A few states sensed an opportunity to attract big banks and pretty much did away with their usury statutes. Soon all of the banks made a run for the border. Any state that wanted a bank to keep employing people in its territory had to do away with its own consumer protections. This effectively ended any kind of usury ceiling for consumers.

This was when getting a credit card became extremely easy. Banks wanted to lure everyone and anyone. They would not only court wealthy customers to pay premiums and interest on huge purchases, as they had in the past. Now they were courting the risky customers who would pay incredible interest. Banks cut the required monthly payment to 2 percent of the balance from 5 percent, hoping that the smaller minimum payment would make you carry more and more of a balance.

They understood perfectly well that America's Joe the Plumbers were overly optimistic about their future prospects. So they offered low introductory "teaser" rates. "The banks don't even have to hide these terms in the fine print," wrote the authors of *Mean Genes*. "They could put them in neon lights on a billboard: YOU'LL PAY SUPER-HIGH INTEREST RATES, BUT NOT FOR SIX MONTHS."

The result is that the burden of the debt that you built up while waiting for your ship to come in went up even faster than the debt itself. According to a 2008 survey by Lending Tree, 20 percent of Americans fear they will never escape their credit card debt and will be stuck with it for the rest of their lives.

What is more, if you have a bank account or a credit card, even if you are a great credit card customer who always pays on time, there is a good chance you've found yourself socked with hidden fees. A Government Accountability study showed that one in every three credit card holders was issued a penalty fee in 2005, an average fee of $34.

"When one-third of all customers pay a penalty," writes Bob Sullivan, author of *Gotcha Capitalism*, "it's no longer a penalty—it's an arbitrary price, a trap designed to catch the maximum amount of people."

Bank fees, not even including credit card fees, take a $32 million bite out of Americans' savings each year. The FDIC reports that bank fee income has soared about 44 percent in the past decade. About half of bank income now comes from fees. Sullivan argues that hidden fees on everything from your cable and cell phone bill to your Internet purchases may be messing up the national inflation rate.

Companies often don't supply surcharges and fee data to the Bureau of Labor Statistics, so when it computes inflation rates, fees aren't reflected. The result is that our national inflation rate is held artificially low.

What is more, if you're broke, you're going to receive the greatest wallop in the form of fees. Can't afford to keep a minimum balance in your checking account? You get a special fee. Accidentally bounce a check? Huge fees. The poorer you are, the more you're going to pay for financial services. This is, of course, simple supply and demand. Why should the bank bother to keep you as a customer, when for the same effort it can cater to multi-millionaire clients?

Such price discrimination happens all the time in a free market. It is a simple fact of life that many products are priced out of reach for low-income consumers, and companies make no effort to cater to them. The difference between bank accounts and other goods and services, however, is that for most products a broke person can find a reasonable alternative. For example, Proctor and Gamble offers Tide laundry detergent for those with money. For the flat broke so-and-so like you, they offer the more modestly priced Gain. Alternatives for the down and out when it comes to financial services range from horrible to very horrible: instant payday loan outfits, title pawn outfits, and check cashing services that take a big bite out of an already modest salary.*

As Ronald T. Wilcox, author of *Whatever Happened to Thrift*, notes, ". . . it is hard to argue the broad social consequences associated with buying Gain. We don't lie awake at night worrying about the poor neighborhood kids who had their jeans washed in Gain rather than Tide. But basic access to capital markets takes on a completely different social dimension. We should worry that there is a sizeable group of people whom banks and other financial institutions find it unprofitable to serve. Such a group almost literally cannot save."

Yet even people with average incomes have been finding it harder to save. One reason is that prices have been secretly going up for years. What do I mean by secretly? Rather than risking sticker shock when costs go up, businesses now tack on hidden fees, obscuring the real price of their goods and services. Once one company uses this strategy,

---

* *The largest pawnshop chain and the largest check-cashing outfit in the United States are both largely financed by some of the largest banks in America.*

competitors will appear to price themselves out of the market by being honest with their consumers.

The most obvious case is in the airline industry. Where most industries offer various products geared toward different income levels (Tide and Gain) airlines have all decided the only way to bring in coach class travelers is to offer the lowest, rock-bottom price. It's as if every restaurant was trying to be McDonald's and no one was trying to be Applebees or an upscale eatery. As if the only shopping option were Wal-Mart and there were no J.C. Penneys or Saks Fifth Avenues.

Since the airlines do nothing to differentiate their brands in our minds, they have all joined in a race to the bottom, first eliminating meals, then snacks, then free movies, then the little blankets and finally letting you check your bags. Instead of giving you these things, they charge you an *a la carte* fee after you've paid for your ticket. It generally doesn't make your flight cheaper, it just makes it seem cheaper, which is the airline's only goal.

A contributor to *The Consumerist* recently wrote in after traveling on Delta Airlines. He noticed that in the travel computer not checking any bags was described as "free!" The contributor, identified only as "Drew," said, "I find it funny that they seem to miss the basic concept behind 'free.' By not checking a bag, I am not being charged. . . . The fact that they offer me nothing, and label it as 'free,' is a bit of a concern."

Even more insidious are the miscellaneous taxes and surcharges, which usually do not appear in the ticket price comparisons in online travel sites until you're ready to check out with your credit card in hand. These hidden costs can sometimes exceed the "price" of the ticket, as

I discovered last year. I tried to book a "$426" international flight and found that the additional "taxes and fees" were $528.

Even the grocery store is not immune to trickery. Many name-brand peanut butter jars are now dented inward at the bottom to reduce the amount the jar holds. It looks as though it is the same size, but it holds two ounces less. Boxes of breakfast cereal are the same height they've always been and look the same on the shelf. But the depth has shrunk, decreasing the box's volume. Rolls of Scott toilet tissue contain the same 1,000 sheets they always have, but the length of the sheet has been trimmed from 4 to 3.7 inches. A "six ounce" can of tuna? It holds five ounces.

Of course, if you're broke, chances are you're paying more for your groceries already. Lower-income families consistently buy small-sized packages of everything because they don't have enough in the week's paycheck to buy the economy size, much less can they be expected to cough up a one-time fee to join a wholesale club.

Harvard Law professor Elizabeth Warren studied years of household spending data collected by the federal government. She adjusted for inflation and matched expenditures by category, clothes, electronics, medicine, food, etc. What she found, wrote James Scurlock in *Maxed Out*, was that the most reliable predictor of whether someone would declare bankruptcy "wasn't the number of credit cards or pairs of shoes in the closet, it was whether or not they were female. And then whether or not that woman had a child. Children were making families go broke!"

Families were not using bankruptcy because they wanted to amass loads of consumer stuff and walk out without paying. It was because Girl Scout cookies and team photos and braces are expensive.

Oh, and if you want to avoid bankruptcy, don't get sick. A more recent study by Harvard University reveals that more than half of all personal bankruptcies in the United States in 2007 were caused by health problems—and that the vast majority of those filers had health insurance.

"For middle-class Americans, health insurance offers little protection. Most of us have policies with so many loopholes, co-payments, and deductibles that illness can put you in the poorhouse," said lead author David U. Himmelstein. "Unless you're Warren Buffett, your family is just one serious illness away from bankruptcy."

More than 90 percent of medically related bankruptcies were caused by high medical bills directly or medical costs that were so high the family was forced to mortgage their home. Another 8 percent went bankrupt because a medical problem caused them to lose income. The authors were not able to track credit-card defaults caused by medical bills, but a 2007 study found that, of low- and middle-income households with credit-card debt, 29 percent used their plastic to pay off medical expenses.*

The purpose of this chapter is not to depress you. It is this: If you feel as though you've been running just to stand still, you should know that this does not mean you're a loser. It means you're normal.

---

*Out of the 192 nations listed in the United Nations World Fact Book, the United States ranks forty-eighth in life expectancy. According to the World Health Organization in terms of disability linked life expectancy, the United States was twenty-fourth out of the twenty-five highly developed nations.

Broke Brokers are Nothing New

According to Sereno Pratt's book *The Work of Wall Street*: "The word *broker* is old. The early English form was *broceur*. By some it is believed to be derived from the Saxon word *broc*, which meant "misfortune," and the first brokers indeed appear to have been men who had failed in business as principals and been compelled to pick up a precarious living as agents."

12

Attention, K-Mart Shoppers: Do You Really Need All That Stuff from China Anyway?

"Man is born free and everywhere is in chain stores."

—GRAFFITO

Fact: When Franklin D. Roosevelt was asked what one thing he would give the Soviet people to teach them about the advantages of American society, he singled out the Sears Roebuck catalog.

Fact: The United States has about forty thousand shopping centers holding nineteen square feet of retail space per citizen, twice that of any country.

Fact: We have more than twice as many shopping centers in the United States as high schools, and we spend more on shoes, jewelry, and watches than on higher education.

You would think at some point you'd be done shopping. At some point you should have everything that you need to get through life, right? With the exception food that rots or gets eaten, most things that we buy last quite a long time. They can last even longer if you patch them up from time to time. If your only guidelines were how many things you already have and how long they will last, you'd rarely have to buy anything at all. Yet somehow you seem to find yourself back in the store or browsing through the listings on Ebay and Amazon.com.

In his 1956 book, *The Life of the Party*, Bennett Cerf told the story of the owner of an industrial plant in Panama who had a dilemma. He had a staff of twenty women who were quite content with their lives. He paid his employees fairly well, and once they had earned enough to meet their needs for several months, they would stop coming to work. He promised them raises and promotions, but they were not interested. They had what they needed, so why work any more? Finally the boss hit on a solution. He collected copies of a one thousand-page mail-order catalog and sent them to all the employees. "They were back at their places," wrote Cerf, "every last one of them—the following Monday."

Not buying may be fine for *you,* but it is not good at all for the people who want to sell you stuff, and the people who want to motivate you to work harder in order to have money to buy more stuff. (Remember the GDP?) Somehow they have to convince you that you need things that you'd never even thought of before—that your life is somehow not complete without an electric eyelash curler, an inflatable floating barbecue for your pool, or Big Mouth Billy Bass, the singing, wall-mounted fish. In short, they have get you to stop wondering whether you should buy something and get you to start thinking about *what to buy*.

By the 1920s, the industrial revolution had transformed American lives. The assembly line and the electrification of everything made workers so productive that the middle class had just about everything it needed. They didn't need to buy anything more. Industrialists began to get nervous. If people had enough, who would buy their stuff? How could their businesses keep growing? That's when they stumbled on a brilliant idea. If Americans didn't need anything more, at least you could make them *want* more.

In 1929, the Herbert Hoover Committee on Recent Economic Changes published a progress report on this new approach to selling: "The survey has proved conclusively what has long been held theoretically to be true, that wants are almost insatiable, that one want satisfied makes way for another. The conclusion is that economically we have a boundless field before us, that there are new wants which will make way endlessly for newer wants, as fast as they are satisfied. . . . Our situation is fortunate, our momentum is remarkable."

Thus was born the concept of the "standard of living." Not only did the modern man (in those days it was a man) go to work to provide basic food, shelter, and security; he was made to feel that he should measure his advancement and progress through his material possessions.

Consumer training starts early in our country. A 1999 study by the Center for a New American Dream, a group that promotes responsible consumption, reveals nearly 65 percent of parents say their own children define self-worth in terms of possessions, and a third of parents report working longer hours to pay for things their kids want. Ad agencies now target the newborn to age three demographic, and in the past six years have increased spending on ads aimed at kids by 50 percent to $2 billion.

Which comes first, the commercial or the product?

In the case of Cap'n Crunch it was the commercial. Jay Ward, the creator of the Rocky and Bullwinkle cartoons, was hired to create a series of commercials featuring a cartoon sailor. When Quaker Oats was satisfied that the commercials would work, they got to work producing the cereal. (Quakers, incidentally, hold simple living as one of the central tenets of their religion.)

Did you know that American homes now contain more stuff than all other households throughout history put together? Our average home size has more than doubled what it was in the 1950s. It's not because we have bigger families. We don't. We have smaller families. We have more stuff. And the punch line? The peak year in which Americans described themselves as "very happy" was 1957.

Fact: The Mall of America has more visitors than Disney World, Graceland, and the Grand Canyon combined.

Fact: The United States spends more than $1,000 billion a year on marketing—about twice what we spend on education, public and private, from kindergarten through graduate school.

The other day I was flipping through television channels. Amid the negative economic stories and the commercials reminding us that times are tough but products are cheap were three shows on the same theme running simultaneously on different networks. What was the theme? Ridding your home of clutter. Oprah Winfrey has made a celebrity of organization expert Peter Walsh. The National Association of Professional Organizers, formed in 1995, has more than 3,700 members. We have so much stuff, we don't know where to put it or what to do with it. It seems it is not difficult to convince us that we need whatever is out there, that it is scarce and valuable, and that we'll regret it for the rest of our lives if we let this opportunity pass us by.

A great example is Scott Bruce and his lunchboxes. Bruce knew that Baby Boomers had created a boom market buying up pop culture items from their childhoods. He knew that if he could come up with a collectible that no one had thought of, he could start hoarding the items and create his own marketing monopoly. Wandering around thrift stores he spotted a metal lunchbox. Lunchboxes were gathering dust in Goodwill stores around the country. They were cheap mass-produced items—an estimated 120 million were stamped out between 1950 and 1970—but they were no longer being made. Most of the boxes were printed with pop culture touchstones like cartoon and TV characters. They were perfect. Bruce started buying them wherever he could find them, usually for a couple of bucks. To make sure people got the message that they were supposed to be *collectible*,* he started publishing a

---

*Collectible *is a strange adjective, because you can* collect *anything—just ask Mildred Sherrer, the sixty nine-year-old who recently won a most boring hobby contest. The retired teacher collects caps from vinegar bottles, all the same brand.*

newsletter, *Hot Boxing*, and followed up with a coffee table book and a price guide based on his collection with values he essentially made up off the top of his head. Having created the market and inflated the prices, he was able to sell the objects he owned at a profit.

Perhaps you know someone with a closet full of baseball cards, Beanie Babies, limited-edition Princess Diana commemorative plates, or what have you. Chances are this person—is it you?—isn't quite sure what's in there, hasn't looked at it in years, but can't bear to part with it, perhaps because he fears the stuff he hoarded because it "might be worth something some day" isn't worth much at all. The dirty little secret of collecting—whether collectibles or clothes or cars—is that imagining having something is far more pleasurable than actually having it. All that consumption is, frankly, a bit disappointing.

If the pursuit of material wealth and consumer stuff fails to bring us the promised happiness, why do we keep going along with a culture that suggests that they do?

Beliefs tend to get passed along if they have some property that facilitates their own transmission, says Daniel Gilbert, author of *Stumbling on Happiness*. Successful ideas do not necessarily need to be true, there just needs to be something about them that gives them a life of their own. For example, if a false belief seems to promote a stable society, it will get passed along as easily as if it were true because stable societies are good transmitters of belief.

"The chair of the Federal Reserve may wake up every morning with a desire to do what the economy wants, but most of us get up with a desire to do what *we* want," Gilbert wrote. "In short, the production of wealth does not necessarily make individuals happy, but it does serve the needs of an economy, which serves the needs of a stable society, which serves a network for the propagation of delusional beliefs about happiness and wealth."

Once such a belief is planted it takes on a life of its own. It continues to spread, because holding it causes us to engage in the very activities that perpetuate it. So this year everybody who is anybody is wearing Nike shoes, and the people who have the Nike shoes seem to be quite happy in them. You don't want to be left out, so you go and buy yourself a brand-new pair of Nike shoes. You walk along as if you've made a conscious and completely personal choice to sport Nike shoes rather than another brand. You have to act that way. Otherwise you'd feel kind of silly about having spent all that money on a swoosh, wouldn't you?

Now the next guy comes along, and because you're so hip and trendy, he realizes that if he is going to be slick like that, he'd better get the Nike shoes. (It could happen.) He's happier than he would have been in bare feet, but not as happy as he thought he would be when he finally had his cool shoes. So this nerd in the Nikes is a little bit bummed out, but the mission of the economy is accomplished. As a matter of fact, now that the dweebs are all wearing the swoosh, you have to go back to the store and get some Air Jordans. You wouldn't dare be lumped in with the pencil pusher in the Nikes. It's just another perfect day for the capitalist system.

Incidentally, those pricey, high-tech athletic shoes actually cause a greater number of injuries than cheap sneakers. Dr. Steven Robbins of Canada's McGill University published this finding in the British Journal of Sports Medicine. He says the over-hyped advertising claims of shock-absorbing, air-cushioned footwear gives wearers a false sense of security, which can make them reckless.

Fact: Forty *billion* mail-order catalogs flood our homes each year, about 150 for each man, woman, and child in the nation.

Fact: The United States is the only country in the developed world without some form of consumption tax.

In his 1979 essay "The Power of Powerlessness," Czech playwright and dissident (and later president of Czechoslovakia) Vaclav Havel described how ordinary citizens perpetuated the Communist system. He imagined the manager of a fruit stand who puts up a poster in his window with the slogan: "Workers of the World, Unite!" The slogan did not express the grocer's opinion, but he put it up anyway. Why? Havel's answer is as applicable to a Nike swoosh as it is to a Communist slogan.

The grocer living under Communism and the kid with a branded T-shirt under a free market system each display their slogans not as an expression of individual belief, but as a message that they want to be accepted into a particular society and do whatever it takes to get along more easily in life.

"The slogan is really a sign," wrote Havel, "and as such it contains a subliminal but very definite message. Verbally, it might be expressed this way: 'I, the greengrocer XY, live here and I know what I must do. I behave in the manner expected of me. I can be depended upon and am beyond reproach. . . . If the greengrocer had been instructed to display the slogan, 'I am afraid and therefore unquestioningly obedient,' he would not be nearly as indifferent to its semantics, even though the statement would reflect the truth."

You've probably noticed that when teenagers decide to become non-conformists they coincidentally choose to *not conform* in exactly the same way their peers are *not conforming*. In the '60s, non-conformists grew their hair long. In the '80s they shaved and shellacked their hair into Mohawks, and in the '90s they pierced something. Nobody decided not to conform by coming to school wearing a tuxedo with giant clown shoes. That would be *real* non-conformity. No, we do what others do, and buy what others buy, so we don't have to feel like a bunch of losers.

"Naturally, the self-seeking consumer finds innumerable people in the marketplace willing to define who he is, for a price," wrote Paul Stiles in *Is the American Dream Killing You?* "If you consider that by the time an individual graduates from high school he has seen well over half a million television commercials, that means he has been told, via this form of media alone, that he is deficient half a million times."

So we choose signals that will identify us as members of a particular social group, whether it is the middle class (a suit), the bohemians (a big flowy patchwork skirt perhaps), bikers (jeans, tattoos, and a leather jacket) or hip-hoppers (Baby Phat and Air Jordan). These days, most of the signals of our identity come in the form of consumer items—fashion, automobiles, MP3 players

The authors of the marketing pep manual *Brand Warfare: 10 Rules for Building the Killer Brand* call these social distinction modern day tribes, ". . . our tribes . . . are manifested by the things we consume. More and more, they are *brand* tribes. . . . The smartest brands take advantage of this mindset by both going after and helping to define a tribe."

Not convinced that brands define us? Consider this observation by Ralph Wagner, a Chicago mutual fund manager: "Harley Davidson is maybe the best brand name in the United States," he said. "Coca-Cola is a good brand name, but people don't tattoo it on their bodies."

Marketers spend millions of dollars and even more creative capital trying to get you to tattoo their name on your body or at least to feel kind of frumpy if you don't get to the Gap. In their competing commercial campaigns, both PC and Mac computers want you to identify completely with their product. "I'm a Mac," says one person. "I'm a PC," says another.

"Brands as smart as this turn into cults," wrote the authors of *Brand Warfare*. "The consumer starts to feel uncomfortable in any other brand.... This is a very pleasant state of codependency that every brand builder should work to achieve."

One thing about all of this brand comparison and covetousness is that we're pretty bad at noticing what our peers actually have. We go over to our friend's house and we spot the HDTV with the Blu-Ray disc player, and we're mesmerized by the clarity of the image. That is just about the most amazing television you have ever seen. Now what do you remember from your visit, the unmatched and chipped flatware at dinner or that HDTV? The HDTV of course. You forget all of the ordinary expected stuff and latch onto the unusual item that pleases you. This gives you an inflated sense of what Bob and Cindy Lou really own, and by extension, what you should have.

The next day you are talking on the phone to your sister in Butte, who just got back from a vacation cruise. She describes in detail the exotic ports and the endless buffets, and you start to wonder why you haven't ever taken a cruise. After you hang up, you forget the part of the conversation where Susan complained about the kids' grades at school and how much overtime she has to put in to get caught up at work. In short, you forget that she was telling you about her vacation because it is unusual, not because it is usual. If you were to look back at your photo albums it would seem as though your own life was one big vacation punctuated by annual Christmas celebrations, because that's what you photograph. It's far from the truth. (Do you have any photographs of yourself at work?)

Over time, with enough of these one-sided observations about your friends' wealth, your idea of what a person from your background should have tends to get a little skewed. This is why, as Ronald T. Wilcox pointed out in *Whatever Happened to Thrift*, those whose income doesn't quite live up to their education level are most likely to have staggering household debt. (A strong argument against getting your PhD in philosophy.)

"This is a socially miserable situation," Wilcox wrote. "The world's finer things are all around you, but you have to struggle financially to socialize with your peers, whose well-educated tastes and preferences are probably quite similar to your own."

So if you've been kicking yourself because having creditors calling at all hours was not supposed to happen to someone with a master's degree, you can stop now. You are *exactly* the type of person it happens to.

As Americans, we do own a lot of stuff—but that stuff also owns us. According to a poll taken by AC Nielsen in May 2005, Americans are the most cash-strapped of any nation. The survey of people in 38 countries found that 28 percent of Americans say they have "no spare cash" after covering their living expenses.

By comparison, only 5 percent of Russians said they had no spare cash at the end of the month.

Monthly earnings of a Russian worker in 2005: An all-time high of 8,655 rubles, or $303 a month.

Earnings of the average American worker in 2005: $926 a *week* gross.

Of those Americans who said they had money "left over" after expenses, the number one use of that money among those surveyed was to *pay off credit cards and other debt.*

Not surprising when you consider that the cumulative personal debt in the United States in 2002 was equal to the gross national product of Great Britain and Russia combined. When you figure debt into the picture, half of America's households have a net worth of $17,800 or less! Still believe everyone is doing better than you are?

Factoid: You're an individual. You don't need Juicy Couture and an iPhone to prove it.

13

A Low Credit Score?
Welcome to the Club

....

*Did you know that the Visa credit card was invented by a
guy named Hock? It's true!*

Sometimes you just have to wait out a rough patch. Robert and Betty
Thumma of Tipton, Iowa, knew this very well. When their silo caught
fire, the couple called the fire department. The firefighters did all they
could, but they couldn't extinguish the blaze. It would seem to go out,
but then the smoldering silo would burst into flames again. The fire
chief decided that the best option was to simply let it burn itself out.
The process took about three weeks.

People who drove past the farm, however, did not know about the
Thumma's conversation with the fire chief. They would ring the door-
bell at all hours of the night to let them know their silo was on fire. The
Thummas couldn't get a wink of sleep. Finally, they put up a big sign
that said, "YES, WE KNOW THE SILO'S BURNING. THANKS."

I was reminded of this story when I was late with a payment to one
of my credit cards. One of the particular frustrations of being self-
employed is that you cannot guarantee your income will arrive on a
certain date. It doesn't always manage to get there at just the time your
credit card wants it. I called the bank to come up with a solution. We set
up an automatic payment to be taken from my checking account in two

weeks time. Before the agent hung up, she told me: "You're still going to get called each day until the payment comes out of your account."

So for two weeks I had a daily conversation with someone in Bangalore, "I already made arrangements, but thanks for calling." (I know the silo's burning, thanks.)

Because of my occasionally tardy payment history several years ago, when my old junker died at the side of the road, I needed a little help. My father came to the rescue and co-signed with me for an auto loan. I regret to say that he passed away shortly thereafter. I sent the death certificate to the company that held my loan and asked to have his name taken off and to list me as the primary borrower. I could go on for several pages recounting the weeks I spent trying to convince the company that the primary obligator was no more, but it would just make me tear my hair out and start crying uncontrollably. To make things short, let's just say that the highlight was when someone called and asked for Albert Lee, because they needed him to fax over another copy of his death certificate.

After all of this effort our exchange went like this:

Finance Company: "We can't put the loan in your name, because your credit is not good enough."

Me: "So you're saying that you would rather have it in the name of a dead person?"

Finance Company: "You don't qualify to be the primary."

Me: "But you do understand that I am more likely to make payments than someone who doesn't exist?"

Finance Company: "We can't take his name off it."

We were at a stalemate, each contemplating the other as if we were from different planets. He was surely wondering why I couldn't understand the simple fact that the rule said I could not be the primary if I had poor credit. It said so right on his screen.

Yet for the life of me I couldn't fathom how having a deceased person primarily responsible for the loan gave the company more security. If the primary borrower failed to pay—which given the circumstances seemed a fairly safe bet—what could they possibly threaten him with? If there is an upside to being dead, it is that you no longer have to worry about your credit score.

Surely someone had made the rule about credit scores in the first place to ensure that the loan was held by someone *who could pay it back*. But the company was sticking to that rule without any regard for changing circumstances. As a result of their own rule, they now were steadfastly determined to have a primary lendee who they knew *for a fact* could not pay. If you enjoy ironic humor, being poor is definitely for you.

Factoid: In each of the past four years more Americans declared personal bankruptcy than graduated from college.

Okay, so you've gotten your report from Freecreditreport.com. Before you contemplate how to tie a noose, think about this. Your credit score, being compiled in far-away computers, is nothing more than a tool used by banks to determine whether or not you'd be a good customer for them. It is not a measure of your worth as a person or a tally of your accomplishments in life. It is not even a measure of your level of personal responsibility. (Incidentally, if you want an actual *free* credit report don't go to freecreditreport.com, which charges you a fee—go to creditkarma.com, which never does.)

If you had never borrowed a thing in your life, had saved up every penny you ever earned, you would not have a good credit score. The best credit score goes not to the most responsible, but to the person most likely to carry enough of a revolving balance to pay a lot of interest to the bank without going under. In fact, in the credit card industry they have a name for people who pay of their credit card balances in full each month. They call them "deadbeats."

So here we all are, measuring our value by how good a prospect we are for a banking salesman. Put that way, it seems like the silliest measure on earth of a person's inherent value and sense of self-worth, doesn't it?*

Here's my alternative suggestion:

Credit Worthiness Score	**Life Worthiness Score**
Payment History 35%	Making a positive
Amount Owed 30%	difference in the world 40%
Length of History 15%	Love you've given 30%
New Credit 10%	Love you've received 30%
Types of Credit Used 10%	

While we're on the subject, can we please stop using the expression "identity theft?" Your identity is the one thing that can never be stolen. Your personal information can be, but that is not who you are.

Sappy, I admit, but I challenge you to come up with your own worthiness score based on what you value most, not how a debt peddler would look at you. Good at sports? Make that a big part of your worthiness score. Good parenting? A huge part of your worthiness score. A hard-working, trustworthy employee at your job? Do volunteer work? Popular among your peers? Active in your church? You get the idea.

Now that you have come up with a very high *life worthiness score* for yourself, want to feel better about your low credit score? Look at your debt as a bank does. The bank is not making moral judgments about you. The bank sees your debt as a valuable product.

Banks buy and sell consumer debt to make money. You are a seller providing a much-needed product to the bank. And if you get behind and they can charge you 30 percent interest, you're really providing something of value. Just think about all those penalty fees they get when you're a day late or have to pay by phone. In 2003 the credit card companies collected $11.7 billion that way, more than half of the total $21.5 billion in fees they collected from cardholders, according to CardWeb, a research firm. They're better off if you don't pay on time.

> **Factoid:** At the time of his death, "King of Pop" Michael Jackson reportedly had a credit score of 563.67 or "poor." Even so, he had been living in a mansion full of expensive art.

A few years ago Elizabeth Warren, the Harvard Law professor who is now chair of the Congressional Oversight Panel created to oversee the Troubled Assets Relief Program, was invited to speak to Citigroup on how to limit losses from charge-offs by customers who fail to pay their bills. Her prescription was simple. If Citigroup would stop lending to people who couldn't afford to repay them, they could cut their charge-off losses in half. After her assessment, a banker stood up and said, "If we cut out those people, we're cutting out the heart of our profits. That's where we make all our money."

About a fifth of those carrying credit card debt pay more than 20 percent in interest.

"I think it is generally understood that those that use the revolving part of the credit card are kind of the sweet spot," Edward Yingling, of the American Bankers Association, admitted to the *New York Times*.

You hear that? Your bankers love you.

Banks don't really want you to save. If they wanted to promote savings they would be plugging savings accounts, not credit cards, on college campuses. During the past decade, bankers made saving money a loser's game. Interest rates were held below the rate of inflation, so anyone who saved actually *lost* money. Better to get one of those gold MasterCards where you can at least get points toward a flight to Tahiti.

And here's something to contemplate—before you started spending money you didn't have, the bank lent you money it didn't have. That's right, it's called "fractional reserve banking," and it works like this: At any one time a bank may have, say, $1 billion in assets, but it will have lent out at least $10 billion, on which it earns interest. It's earning interest on money the bank doesn't actually own, based on a prediction of how much your money will nab when it's invested, not on how much is actually in its deposit accounts. (Don't you wish you could do that?) Call it a faith-based initiative.

Most money these days does not come in the form of pieces of paper with numbers on it. It comes in the form of computer transactions between banks. When you get a loan from the bank to buy a new car, chances are the bank is not going to hand you a sack of pennies. Instead they put a number into your account in the computer. Where does that money come from? Nowhere! Isn't that great? They just decide you can have another $5,000 worth of digits in your account. It is not taken from another customer's account or from a vault. Of course, the money isn't entirely fictional. The bank has at least a tenth of the amount it lent out to customers in its reserves.

But where did *that* currency come from? Here's where it gets interesting. You take your loan and spend it on a quality previously owned vehicle. The used car dealer takes your check and deposits it into his bank account. From his bank's perspective, this is plain old money, not a loan. Their deposits increase, and the amount of corresponding money they can lend out increases.

"Each and every time a bank makes a loan, new bank credit is created—new deposits—brand new money," said former Governor of the Central Bank of Canada Graham Towers.

Viewed this way, the humble debtor, not the corporate CEO, is the driving engine of the entire economy. Sir Albert Feaveryear's economic history, *The Pound Sterling*, shows that banks created and supplied about 40 percent of the money stock in the eighteenth century to nations such as Britain, France, and the United States. By the mid-nineteenth century this had risen to 60 percent. Today banks supply between 90–97 percent of the new money.

"Thus," wrote Michael Rowbotham in *The Grip of Death*, "the supply of money depends upon people going into debt, and the level of debt within an economy is no more than a measure of the amount of money that has been created. . . . This empty spiral of numbers based upon numbers is the heart of the financial system upon which economies throughout the entire world are built."

The bank couldn't put you in hock to them if they weren't in hock to you first. So don't worry about what the bankers think of you. They're on shakier footing than you are. They just have nicer suits.

If that doesn't cheer you up, try this. You know who else was in over his head? Abraham Lincoln. Before he got into politics, Honest Abe borrowed some money to open a store. His career as a merchant was an utter failure. The store went under, and the future president could not emancipate himself from his debts. He needed a job and fast, so he campaigned for the state legislature. He won the election, but after the victory celebration, he discovered that his horse was missing. The sheriff had taken the horse, the bridle, saddle, and all of Lincoln's possessions, and put them up for auction to cover the debts. But the sum total of Lincoln's property was still not enough to cover it. It took Lincoln seventeen years to repay what he owed and become solvent.

Lincoln once told a friend: "That debt was the greatest obstacle I have ever met in my life; I had no way of speculating, and could not earn money except by labor, and to earn by labor eleven hundred dollars besides my living seemed the work of a lifetime. There was, however, but one way. I went to my creditors and told them that if they would let me alone I would give them all I could earn over my living as fast as I could earn it."

According to his law partner, William Herndon, Lincoln was still sending money back to his New Salem, Illinois, creditors two decades later as a member of Congress.

You wouldn't judge Abraham Lincoln by his credit score would you? Don't judge yourself that way either.

THINGS TO BE THANKFUL FOR

You're surely better off than Mr. William Stern, who filed the largest bankruptcy in British history in 1978. Before he went bust, the property mogul bragged that banks competed to loan him money. (This was in the 1970s, before those Lending Tree commercials hit the airwaves.) At age 43, Stern had managed to rack up liabilities in excess of £100,000,000 against assets of £10,070. Hearing the case in London Bankruptcy Court, Mr. Alan Sales was unfazed. "This bankruptcy has been described as the world's biggest," he said, "but really it is a very ordinary bankruptcy with noughts at the end." It might not impress the collections department, but you'll feel better.

14

Broke Person's Hero: Father Jeremiah O'Callaghan

But love ye your enemies, and do good, and lend, hoping for nothing again, and your reward shall be great

—LUKE 6:35

If you're paying 28 percent interest to your credit cards you can possibly blame your circumstances on another heroic failure, the Irish priest Father Jeremiah O'Callaghan, who lost his ministry, his paycheck and even his country in a quixotic battle against the practice of usury.

Today we think of usury as charging *excessive* interest on a loan, but originally usury referred to any interest on a loan at all. In 1819, when the popular priest was thirty-nine years old, he heard two elderly clerics debating the issue of usury and whether the church should condemn the practice.

Daniel Burke, the priest who argued against usury, was out-gunned by his more articulate adversary, but O'Callaghan went away convinced that he had been right. Hadn't Jesus himself said in Luke 6:35, "Lend, hoping for nothing again?"

Too many people had seen their dreams of a better life scuttled against the rocks of mounting debt and excessive interest, and giving out anything but generosity of spirit was bad for the soul. O'Callaghan had found his calling. Thus he began preaching eloquently on the subject. One day he was asked to administer last rites to a merchant who charged interest on money owed to him for grain. O'Callaghan convinced the old man that the gates of heaven would be closed to him unless he repented and returned the interest he had taken to his debtors. The merchant was won over, and he ordered the executors of his will to give the money back.

For O'Callaghan it was a spiritual triumph, and a small step toward abolishing the sin of usury. And what did he receive as a reward for his victory? He was rebuked by his superior, Bishop Coppinger of Cloyne and Ross—who had gotten an earful from the heirs—and removed from his post.

O'Callaghan protested his firing. He pointed out, quite rightly, that the official church position was that usury was a sin. Surely the Vatican would see that saving men's souls was more important than keeping them comfortable with their sinful habits.

But, as Christian historian Ray C. Petry noted in a biography of St. Francis of Assisi, "Jesus' legacy of the poor life was, in time, to prove a challenging, if somewhat embarrassing, bequest to his followers.... All too many religious associations began with Jesus' injunctions and then rationalized them to suit the pressing demands of worldly circumstances."

While the church was not ready to reverse its stand on the issue of usury, it was too pragmatic to be comfortable with a priest who branded some of the most influential and prominent citizens as sinners. O'Callaghan followed the letter of church doctrine right out of a job.

The Vatican refused to answer his letter, but news of it inspired Coppinger to forbid the troublemaking priest from saying mass. O'Callaghan fled to America, where he was sure the Bishops would be more sympathetic to his orthodox interpretation of church law. Anyway, he knew that they were short on priests in New York and they would pretty much have to put him in the pulpit. But wherever he went, as soon as the bishops got a look at O'Callaghan's record, they turned him away.

Having no luck in the United States, O'Callaghan boarded a ship for Canada. By the time he arrived he was hungry and sick. The winter was harsh, and with no church offering him a home, O'Callaghan was forced to rely on the charity of a sympathetic priest. A priest without a church, O'Callaghan spent the winter writing a book with the pithy title, *Usury or Lending at Interest... Proved to be Repugnant to the Divine and Ecclesiastical Law and Destructive to Civil Society.*

Finally, O'Callaghan received some good news. The Holy See had replied to his letter at long last. He was instructed to return to Ireland and to make peace with Bishop Coppinger. Finally he would be back in his home, and back to his calling, ministering to the people of Ireland.

O'Callaghan bundled up sixty copies of his book, boarded a ship, and headed home. Coppinger, however, had a different view of the Vatican's instructions.

"You are commanded to come to me," he said, "but I am not commanded to receive you."

Once again, O'Callaghan was left out in the cold. He could not believe the church would turn its back on him for teaching Catholic doctrine as it was written. He decided to take his case directly to Rome.

On the way O'Callaghan experienced what should have been a great change in his fortunes. As he passed through London he left a copy of his book at the office of William Cobbett, the political activist and journalist. As O'Callaghan pressed on to Rome, Cobbett read the manuscript and agreed completely with its theme. He didn't know how to reach its author, but he wasted no time publishing the book anyway. (You could do that in those days.)

By the time O'Callaghan made it to Rome to plead his case, Bishop Coppinger had read a copy of the book. He told the Vatican that O'Callaghan was a parasite, living off the generosity of the Vatican, while earning hefty royalties from his book. The Vatican was tired of the bickering and embarrassed by O'Callaghan's insistence on actually preaching a doctrine that it had abandoned by default.

So how do you stop someone from speaking out against capitalism? Cut off his capital. The church stopped O'Callaghan's allowance, and send him packing. With no pulpit, no community, and no money to sustain him, the articulate minister, who once inspired a lender to repent, was forced to become a borrower. With only a few pennies in his pocket, he relied on the generosity of passersby to pay his fare back to London.

That was the inauspicious end of one man's quest to remind the church of its own doctrine. O'Callaghan and Cobbett had a little commercial success with the usury book, and O'Callaghan managed to eventually find a home and a church in rural New England. But he failed to turn the tide of public sentiment against lending with interest—and completely failed in preventing you from selling your soul to MasterCard.

15

An Honest Day's Work: A Cultural View of Financial Values

"The age of the self-made man was also the age of the broken man. . . . This 'American sense' looked upon failure as a 'moral sieve' that trapped the loafer and passed the true man through. Such ideologies fixed blame squarely on individual faults, not extenuating circumstances."

—SCOTT A. SANDAGE, *BORN LOSERS*

George S. Parker, the founder of Parker Brothers with his sibling Charles, was born in 1867. He was the son of a merchant, and in his spare time he liked to get together with friends to play chess, checkers, dominoes, and the board games that existed then, most of which were designed to teach religious and moral values. You won by making correct ethical choices and a few lucky moves.

Parker was more interested in a game about another kind of value: money. He created "The Game of Banking," the first in which the object was to become the richest player on the board. Parker Brothers would eventually go on to release one of the most popular board games of the modern era, "The Game of Life," which had several versions over the years. There was one in which players could literally sell their children back to the bank when they become broke. (Last year, Hasbro announced it would be launching a new edition of "The Game of Life" called "Twists and Turns," which replaces play money with a Visa-branded card. It will be the perfect Christmas gift for the consumer in training.)

Even Monopoly, the quintessential game of capitalism, was modeled on a Quaker-created board game. The "Landlord's Game," patented by Elizabeth Magie of Maryland, was designed to satirize capitalism and discourage property speculation. Along with familiar spaces like banks, railroads, utilities, and jail there was a public park and a "Mother Earth" at one of the corners.

The shift from being the most pious to the most wealthy to win mirrored the change in the bedtime stories we told to adults.

Before the age of the self-made man, people were born into a certain social stratum and that was it. If you were the son of a merchant, or artisan, or king, it defined your place in the world forever. Because you had no way to change it, there was no shame associated with it. People were seen as part of an interdependent system in which social status was pre-ordained. The measure of a person's "worth" was his moral correctness.

"For centuries," writes Alain de Botton in *Status Anxiety*, "economic orthodoxy held that it was the working classes that generated society's financial resources—which the rich then dissipated through their taste for extravagance and luxury."

De Botton dates the beginning of the end of this view to 1723, when a London physician named Bernard Mandeville published *The Fable of the Bees*. Its premise, now very familiar, was that the wealthy, by spending, allowed those who they paid to survive. Wealth in this model is seen as flowing down from the top rather than growing up from the ground.

"In early America," wrote Scott Sandage in *Born Losers*, "fear of failure loomed largest on Sunday. Monday morning dawned about the year 1800. By then failure meant an entrepreneurial fall from grace. . . . By mid-century, success or failure often depended on the story a man could tell about his own life—or that others could tell about him. Bureaucratic institutions such as credit-rating agencies, bankruptcy courts, and charity bureaus added their own form of discipline to that marketplace. Such agencies operated by classifying people, putting them into boxes tagged 'failure' or 'success,' 'winner' or 'loser.' Life stories took on tangible consequences for both the financial security and social worth of an individual."

As we moved into the twentieth century, our cultural identities shifted from "citizens" to "consumers." As consumers, our primary civic duty has been to support businesses by shopping, which has led some to speculate that Capitalism has become our theology and the Market has become our God. Milton Friedman, long-time economics professor at the University of Chicago and principle architect of what some people call "Free Market Fundamentalism," once referred to himself as "a country preacher spinning a sermon of salvation."

Yet if the market is a god, it is, according to Thomas Frank, "the god that sucked." Writing for the literary magazine *The Baffler,* he said, "This is a deity of spectacular theological agility, supported by a priesthood of millions . . . all united in the conviction that, no matter what, the market can't be held responsible. When things go wrong, only we are to blame. After all, they remind us, every step in the economic process is a matter of choice. We choose Ford over Dodge and Colgate Total over Colgate Ultra-Whitening."

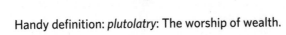

Handy definition: *plutolatry*: The worship of wealth.

The unquestioned faith that hard work equals wealth and success is interpreted to mean that poverty can only be the result of laziness. As we also equate laziness with selfishness and greed—not pulling your weight—we end up with a belief system in which those with excess wealth, even inherited wealth, are seen as more hard working and contributing more to society. Those who have the most are generous. Those who have the least are greedy. Many people cling to this belief even when there are counterexamples everywhere. Pop quiz: Who do you think of as a harder worker? A single mother working two minimum wage jobs or Paris Hilton?

We would very much like to hold on to our belief that the world is fair. We would also like to believe that in a fair world, the person who works the hardest or contributes the most to society will receive the greatest rewards. Keeping those values in mind, take a look at Paris Hilton's latest magazine cover. *People* may have a lot to say about the foibles of Paris Hilton, but *failure* is not a word that ever comes up. Wealth, even inherited wealth, shields you from the word *failure.*

With the focus of our admiration so divorced from our ethic of hard work, we've come to the unfortunate conclusion that the God of the Market will forgive us all our sins, as long as we do His work, i.e., make lots of money. At least that is what David Callahan has argued in his book *The Cheating Culture*.

"In principle, few Americans embrace the idea that 'might makes right,'" he wrote. "In practice, this idea now flourishes across our society, and much of the new cheating is among those with the highest incomes and social status. . . . This hubris is only partly founded on the kind of delusions made possible by a culture that imputes moral superiority to those who achieve material success."

Pointing to the Enron and other corporate scandals, Callahan argues that cheating has become so pervasive that people who want to take the high road often feel they will be disadvantaged if they play by the official rules rather than the *real* rules.

This seems especially true among young people. In 1996, the Good Work Project began studying dozens of young workers as they encountered situations that tested their ethics and values. The young people regularly made moral compromises with the justification that once they had become established they could serve as paragons of moral value—but they had to get established first.

The researchers, who published their findings in the book *Making Good*, illustrated this point with the story of an aspiring actress named Meg who, against her instincts, took a role that portrayed Asian-American women in a stereotypical light.

"And ultimately, like many of the journalists and geneticists we interviewed, she indicated that she thought the ends justified the means. In this case, taking sub-standard roles that could bring greater opportunities would allow her to gain power in the theater community and ultimately to realize her most cherished values. Meg contended that as she gained influence, she would be in a better position to undermine racial stereotypes. For her, the expectation of taking a principled stand in the future warranted compromises in the present."

But if there is one thing we know about the American Dream it is this—it is a moving target. You will never have arrived. There will be no magic moment when you feel you have gotten all you could want, that your position is completely secure, and that you can now stop striving. So if you're waiting to "arrive" before your ethics kick in, you are not likely to ever live up to your highest values.

We Pause for a Commercial Announcement: I Pledge Allegiance...

Every day, American schoolchildren start their day with an oath: "I pledge allegiance to the flag of the United States of America. . . ." You know the rest. Appropriately enough for the champion of capitalism and free markets, the Pledge of Allegiance was the result of a publicity campaign. In order to build circulation, the children's magazine *The Youth's Companion* ran a contest in 1892 for the best patriotic-sounding loyalty oath.

Want more? A Ten Commandments monument on the grounds of the Texas capital in Austin, the inspiration of a U.S. Supreme

Court hearing, was not placed there originally as a symbol of legal justice or even as an expression of piety. It was created as an advertisement for a movie. When Paramount Pictures was about to release the film *The Ten Commandments*, Cecil B. DeMille teamed up with the Fraternal Order of Eagles on a publicity scheme. The studio sponsored the construction of several thousand Ten Commandments monuments throughout the country.

16

Thrift, Horatio. Thrift.

....

"The very word thrift tells its own tale, being derived from the word 'to thrive.'"

—JOHN LUBBOCK, *THE USE OF LIFE*, 1894

These days, when we talk about thrift, we're usually thinking about deprivation of some kind. A thrifty person reuses string, wears shoes until they have holes in them, and haggles over the price of bulk flour. But the original meaning of *thrift* was quite different. *Thrift* meant prosperity and growth. It was most often applied to nature, or used as a metaphor for the growth of healthy plants. A healthy garden was a *thrifty* garden. A sunflower as high as an elephant's eye was *thrifty*. In that spirit, you should not look upon economic thrift as deprivation, but as your means to grow and thrive.

Factoid: The arm of the Treasury Department that regulated many lenders in the subprime mortgage market is called "The Office of Thrift Supervision."

Sitting by my telephone is a lacquered piece of curved wood that holds a dowel and a roll of adding machine paper. The two sides of this object are just the width and height to support the paper roll, which presents a bit of a usability issue. It's wide enough for the paper, but not wide enough for a hand holding a pen. This wouldn't be a problem except the "roll-a-note" is supposed to make it easier to jot down phone messages. To actually take a phone message using a roll-a-note, you need to pull the paper all the way past the base and its little plastic stopper—I think it's supposed to be a paper cutter of some kind—and write on the table itself. This, of course, defeats the purpose of the roll-a-note all together. It would be much simpler to keep a spiral notebook or a small box with paper scraps in it. So why do I keep this wreck of a labor-saving device? Because I made it. It was the first actual thing I made in my seventh-grade "industrial arts" class.

Making useful items is not something that comes naturally to me. And *industrial* and *arts* are two words that I still think should never be in the same sentence, let alone the same course name. But it was a requirement, along with home ec. I put on the plastic goggles that left a line in my cheeks, and I risked my fingers pushing the pine into the jig saw and tracing the rounded pattern to create the sides. I filed it down and watched the sawdust fly. I even melted the sides of the little plastic stopper/cutter so that it could be folded over and fitted to the creation's base. After all that effort, I was not going to discard it over a little thing like its being completely useless.

It is still in my house along with my home ec projects, a throw pillow made out of two washcloths and some yarn, and a fairly unsightly and uneven duffel bag with a draw string. I originally sewed the two sides together, and had to start again from scratch.

A friend of mine keeps a special incense burner in her closet. It is "special" in the "isn't that special" sense. My friend maintains the sort of earthy life style that is normally well suited to candles and incense burners. This burner, however, is something else. It is a black and sparkly giant sphinx. When you burn an incense cone in its base, the smoke rises and billows out of its ears and mouth like some fantasy monster.

"It is extremely tacky," my friend says of the unwanted gift, "But she meant it from her heart." So there the sphinx sits, in the closet ready to be put on display when the friend comes to visit. "Thank god we have lots of notice. And we won't even go into the matching vests and bandanas that (my friend's) aunt hand sews for us. Oh boy!" [Identities obscured to protect the gift givers.]

Roll-a-notes and sphinx burners may not be the most useful things we own, but here's the thing—we still own them. Plastic toys, DVDs, and clothes may come and go, but the matching hand-sewn vest stays in its special place in the closet.

These days we hear a lot of news stories about the magnitude of our consumer waste. When we talk about our trash, it is usually a big picture of the municipal waste stream. It comes in the form of a new story about a barge full of trash circling Islip with nowhere to land, or a television special like National Geographic's *Human Footprint*, which lays out all of our discards in staggeringly large piles. The big picture is so vast, that it is hard to assimilate it. It is too great for us to take it in personally.

The news stories usually go on to recommend some small change we can make to stem the tide, recycling plastic or buying compact fluorescent bulbs, for instance. Sometimes the stories talk about the way things used to be. They remind us that in days gone by hearty farmers didn't let anything go to waste. Advice manuals from the nineteenth century offer tips for "turning" old sheets when they got thin and worn by cutting them down the middle and sewing the outer edges together and mending broken china by tying it up and boiling it in milk. Colonial homes would use chipped and broken plates until they were too small to hold food. You are left with the impression that people in the old days were much more resourceful and creative and had better values than we have today.

Why is it so easy for us in the twenty-first century to cast useful things away? One reason is that we no longer make the stuff. Thanks to mass production, advanced delivery systems, and globalization, very little of what we have is made by hand, and most of what we buy is not even made in factories in this country.

If you lived a century ago, just about anything you owned would be either painstakingly made by hand yourself, or by a friend or relative. Your community would be so small that you would know the guy who made the shoes for your horse. You would know the guy who made your butter churn. You would know the cobbler who made your shoes. People a century ago knew exactly where their stuff came from and how much effort it took to create it.

Of course their thriftiness had other causes as well—they wanted to preserve limited resources and money—but one that we rarely think about is how reluctant you would be to chuck a pillow crocheted by mom, a table made by Uncle Joe, or a skirt you sewed yourself. The personal attachment to stuff made everyone conservative about throwing things away.

"Repair ideas come more easily to people who make things," Susan Strasser noted in *Waste and Want: A Social History of Trash.* "If you know how to knit or do carpentry, you also understand how to mend a torn sweater or repair a broken chair. You can appraise the materials and evaluate the labor of the original maker. . . . Indeed, mending and restoring objects often requires even more creativity than the original production."

Somewhere along the line we lost our authentic connection to things as the result of our creative and manual labor, and that has made it easier for us to send the stuff out from Islip on a garbage scow, and the meaning of *conservatism* (as in *conserving*) got a bit lost.

"Deliberate obsolescence in all its forms—technological, psychological, or planned—is a uniquely American invention," wrote Giles Slade in *Made to Break.* "Not only did we invent disposable products, ranging from diapers to cameras to contact lenses, but we invented the very concept of disposability itself."

In the late 1800s, King C. Gillette was a traveling cork salesman struggling to make a living. His luck changed after a discussion with a friend named William Painter, who'd made a fortune with a new type of bottle closure—the bottle cap. Painter gave Gillette some novel advice that is now conventional wisdom: to thrive in business, you should produce something that could be used a few times and then thrown away. Gillette went away and invented the disposable razor. The concept of getting a lifetime of use from a product was starting to erode.

Amazingly enough, during World War I, when the U.S. Treasury Department initiated a thrift and savings campaign, merchants fought tooth and nail against it. In 1917, stores in every city started displaying signs with slogans like "Business as Usual. Beware of Thrift and Unwise Economy." New York retailers created the "National Prosperity Committee,"which printed signs reading, "Buy What You Need Now!"

Disposables really started to get a toe-hold after the war. In the roaring twenties, marketers began to use the argument that disposable products were much more hygienic and convenient, and an increasingly urban nation was convinced. Disposability gave all of us the ability to have brand-new items all the time, and to achieve levels of cleanliness and convenience once reserved for nobles. The ability to waste made us little kings. First came Band-Aids and sanitary napkins, which led to paper cups and plates, TV dinners in aluminum trays, and all manner of throw-aways, right up to today's disposable dusters and mop heads.

In 1923, General Motors led the charge to a new era of product obsolescence. Previously products became obsolete when there was a major technological advance; you replaced your steel pots with iron ones or your car with a crank start to one with an electric starter. But GM bet that people with perfectly functional automobiles could be lured into the showroom by a new cosmetic design. Coming out with a new model each year and getting people to buy out of fashion was a huge success and spread through the manufacturing world like wildfire.

The Great Depression provided the next great leap in product obsolescence. Because economic pressures were so great, manufacturers were forced to use substandard materials in their products. It was the only way to keep their prices within reach of the strapped consumer. After a short time, manufacturers began to realize that churning out cheap products that conk out after a couple of years meant that people had to buy more often, and they sold more stuff. Thus was born "planned obsolescence," a variety of methods that force you to upgrade on a regular basis, culminating with the *pièce de résistance*, computer technology. As Oliver Strimpel of the now-defunct Boston Computer Museum said, "Men find new technology appealing even if they don't know what they want it for." Here's your upgrade to version 3.1.

Research has shown that the lifespan of goods has been falling for years. In an era of mounting credit card debt, cheap consumer goods designed to be quickly obsolete are just about the only products that stand a chance. It is not that consumers do not want to think long term and get something that will last a while; it's just that they cannot afford to do so. You can't get the long-lasting, high-quality product you want today because you are still burdened with paying for the cheap appliances you bought with plastic five years ago. So instead of the expensive item you know will last longer, you get a cheaper one and throw it out and get a new one in a couple of years. In the end, having a vacuum cleaner costs the same, but you have to buy it twice. You're in essence paying for it over time, as you pay for everything else, and creating a heap of waste in the process.

Fair Enough

An ad man for John Wanamaker, one of the pioneers of the modern department store, was called upon to write a slogan for some neck-ties that had been reduced in price from a dollar to 25 cents. The ad man looked at the ties and asked the buyer, "Are they any good?" The buyer shrugged and admitted they were not. The ad man though for a moment and then came up with the following copy: "They are not as good as they look, but they are good enough at 25 cents." The demand was so great that Wanamaker's had to keep restocking the cheap ties.

17

The Poor Person's Shopping Mall: The World of Secondhand Goods

*Another garage sale opens every fifteen seconds in the United States. Although no one can say for sure, garage sales are estimated to take in about $3 billion a year. **That's a billion with a b.***

As Americans, we've been pretty well trained to equate the ability to shop with our sense of well-being. The good news is that there are some classic places for the broke to go and enjoy consumerism—the world of secondhand goods.

Of course you'll want to steer clear of the high-priced consignment shops, antique stores, and the "collectibles" at estate sales. (Although estate sales can be great for the types of items you need and estate agents don't want to deal with—small toys, leftover shampoos and soaps. . . . I once got three full bags of groceries at an estate sale for $17.)

Sure, that Coach or Prada purse is appealing. It may not look any better than the one you got at the Salvation Army, but it does scream out "Look, I'm rich!"

Would it help you to know that a lot of those luxury clothing brands are made in the same Chinese and Cambodian factories as your Wal-Mart duds? It used to be that those high-ticket items were lovingly crafted by hand, but that is simply not so any more. You can get the same luxury results by buying the stuff at discount prices and shouting "Look, I'm rich!" verbally.

Marc Jacobs, creative director of Louis Vuitton, the world's largest luxury goods company, defines luxury this way: "For me, luxury is about pleasing yourself, not dressing for other people."

Who is more likely to dress with little regard for trends than a broke person? Now is the time to develop a quirky fashion sense. Unique is chic. Aren't you just a little too cool to dress up in cookie-cutter, mass-produced fashions anyway? The Goodwill Store has its half-price sale on Wednesday. Go for it.

Cultivating an idiosyncratic sense of low-culture chic can work for you just as it did for the Trachtenburg family of Seattle. The family was making a modest living running a dog walking service. By night patriarch Jason was an amateur musician playing competent but not particularly original sets at open-mic nights. All of that changed when they stumbled upon a $5 slide projector at a garage sale. Along with the projector was a set of slides from somebody's 1959 trip to Japan. The slides captured Jason's imagination, and he wrote a song: "Mountain Trip to Japan, 1959."

Now with a hook, the family dubbed themselves the Trachtenburg Family Slideshow Players. The result is a nerd-chic marriage of They Might Be Giants and the Partridge Family that Trachtenburg described to the San Francisco Chronicle as ". . . an indie, vaudeville, conceptual art, pop-rock, family slideshow band." Decked out in colorful retro garage sale cast-offs, they have gained an international cult following. Their success is a triumph of the unusual over the well-packaged and mass-produced.

"It worked within our economic means," Trachtenburg told Bruce Littlefield, author of *Garage Sale America*, "And came directly from our garage sale lifestyle. By acquiring our slides, our clothes, our bric-a-brac from other people's unwanted castoffs, it's the least environmental impact we can have. If we can make art out of the excesses of our overwhelming culture, then it's highly evolved."

Of course, resale isn't only for the penniless. Al Hoff, a self-described middle-class thrift store shopper, writes all about her adventures trying to find the most quirky items in her 'zine and book, *Thrift Score*. She spends a bit of time wrestling with her conscience about buying low-priced Salvation Army duds when she could afford to shop for the new stuff and leave the cast-offs for the poor.

If you're broke, you should have no such qualms, but even if your level of broke-ness is such that you have to save up for the big-screen TV, you should still not feel guilty that you're "stealing" from the less fortunate. The basis of this argument is a faulty one. *We have no shortage of stuff in our country.* Shop flea markets, thrift shops, and garage sales to your heart's content. We're not going to run out any time soon.

As a matter of fact, an article in the London *Sunday Times* notes that charity shops are all but overwhelmed by clothing cast-offs. We discard last season's fashions, barely worn, in a tsunami of donations.

"Clothing is now given in such huge quantities to British charities that they can't sell it all in the shops," said Lucy Norris, co-curator of a museum exhibit that traced the odyssey of clothes dumped in Oxfam clothing banks.

And this is in England—imagine what we're dealing with in the king of consumer cultures, the United States of America. To make room in the thrift store, a lot of the clothing is shipped to Eastern Europe, Africa, and Asia, where it is either sold whole or organized into color-coded stacks and shredded, pulped and respun into yarn to make cheap blankets. Now there is a worry that U.S. and European second-hand exports are so voluminous that they are threatening the local garment trades in developing nations. From 1985 to 1992, 51 out of 72 Zambian clothing firms closed, partly due to this kind of competition. What if we could get out of the cycle of overproduction and buying and re-buying goods all together? If there is something you want, surely there is someone out there who is about ready to chuck just such an item into a bin. What if you could connect up and just trade the things you can't use? Enter barter networks and the gift economy.

You have a talent or skill and another person has an item you need. You could go out and work for a third person, wait for that person to pay you money, and then trade the money for the item. Or you could offer your skill to the person with the item directly. The easiest way to barter is to deal with contacts you already have: friends, family, business associates. But the Internet has made it much easier to connect with strangers who are looking for what you've got. Kyle MacDonald of Montreal used a Craigslist barter board as a launch site for his successful quest to trade up from a single red paper clip to a house. In a year and fourteen swaps, MacDonald worked his way up to a pen that looked like a fish to a handmade doorknob, to a camp stove, to a 100-watt generator, to an "instant party kit," to a snow-mobile, to an afternoon with rock star Alice Cooper, and finally a KISS snow globe, which he traded to Corbin Bernsen, who it seems is a die-hard snow globe collector, for a paid role in a movie, which Mac-Donald finally exchanged for the house, as well as a key to the city of Kilpling, Saskatchewan.

Of course, to achieve those kinds of results, it helps to have gift for self-promotion and the ability to make your quest into a cause celebre. Most of us have to settle for more modest bartering of goods and services, trading an old paperback you've read for one you haven't, for example. (See the resources section in the back of the book for a list of barter sites.)

Freecycle is a growing phenomenon that uses the social network of the Internet to connect people who have stuff they don't want with people who want stuff they don't have. Deron Beal launched the network in Tucson in 2003. Beal was then working for a nonprofit group that combined recycling with job training. Freecycle began as a modest e-mail list among friends. A newspaper article on his list bumped membership overnight from 80 to 800. Since then it has ballooned to 4,000 networks operating in 75 countries with 3.5 million members.

You can also find lots of great free castoffs at your local dump. Many waste facilities have special areas where useful items are set aside and offered free to whoever wants them. The practice of picking up other people's cast offs seems to be especially well-regarded in thrifty New England. Wrote Philip Simmons in *Learning to Fall*, " There's a saying that you know you're really from New Hampshire if you leave the dump with more than you came with."

Most waste disposal facilities offer various recycling services. You can, for example, take compost for your garden. For businesses there are materials exchange services in which organizations can list the excess materials they cannot use, and exchange them with other businesses. Look up "materials exchange service" in your favorite search engine.

Everybody Whang Chung Tonight: Creativity on a Shoestring Budget

The colonists of New Haven used shoestrings instead of buckles. The strings were cut from rawhide and called "whang." In the nineteenth century, a fellow appropriately named "Shoestring Pratt" of Randolph, Massachusetts, devised a no cost business for himself. He went around to shoemakers' factories and asked if he could take away their trash—the scraps of leather that were left over when shoes were made. Next Pratt came up with a way of cutting the scrap leather, pulling the strands straight, rolling them in their own fat and cutting them into standard lengths to make whang. He then sold the shoemakers back the product he had made out of their own garbage.

18

Alternative Identity— It's Just That Easy Being Green

....

"What if the greenest people on the planet were people with dirty jobs? . . . You don't see it because they're too busy making a living doing what they do. There are more important things to them than saving the planet—namely making a living and taking care of their family."

—MIKE ROWE, HOST OF THE TELEVISION SERIES *DIRTY JOBS*

Now that we have talked about the trend toward planned obsolescence, let's talk about the results: The world's largest man-made structure is no longer the Great Wall of China: It is the Fresh Kills landfill in New York. Before it closed in March 2001, New York deposited 2 billion tons of garbage at the landfill on Staten Island. It is twenty times the size of the Great Pyramid at Giza, Egypt, and rises to a height of 155 feet, the highest point on the Eastern Seaboard south of Maine. It overtook the Great Wall of China as the largest man-made object in 1991.

Even the summit of the world's tallest mountain is not litter free. Mountaineers leave oxygen bottles, gas cartridges, and plastics near the top of Mt. Everest as they make their way to the summit. It is estimated that there is about four to five tons of discarded oxygen bottles and other assorted trash strewn along the world's tallest peak. This is on top of a ton of trash that mountain climbers have already risked their lives to bring down.

The good news is that a lot of the things you do to save money and the things you do to be a green look very similar. Greens fold envelopes inside out and reuse them. Greens pack their school lunches in reusable totes so they don't have to buy wasteful plastic bags. If they do use plastic bags, they wash them out and use them again. Greens make things out of old packaging and rescue things from the landfill. Greens like to grow their own food and make their own clothes. Greens find ways to reduce their consumption of water and electricity, both of which can also save money.

The benefit of defining yourself as a green is that you can turn embarrassment over broken dishes and patched-up furniture into moral triumph. Show them the extremes to which you will go to reduce waste and save the planet. Your detractors will go a bit quiet and start to mumble something about compact florescent bulbs. You can hold your head high and turn your inability to get new stuff into the moral triumph of using your old stuff until it crumbles to bits. You will save money, demonstrate your commitment to a sustainable future, and have the opportunity to stretch your imagination.

A lot of people approach going green as just another consumer habit. They buy the latest green gear from Whole Foods and the Real Good catalog and then dump their wasteful non-green old stuff into the landfill. Not only is this ironic—don't you think?—it can be much more expensive than not going green at all. Use your creative capital, not your financial capital, and find new uses for old things. Being green doesn't have to be a solitary endeavor. It works best, in fact, if you get your family and friends on board.

Ohio high school teacher Jennifer Hunter describes some of the things her family did to save money, things that they could just as easily define as eco-friendly activities: "I can remember how exciting it was as a child to 'camp out' in the family room and sleep in sleeping bags because my parent had closed off the front of the house to conserve on the heating bills," she says. "But, my personal favorites were the 'no electricity nights.' My parents would turn off all the electric appliances in the house (except the refrigerator), turn down the furnace, and turn off the lights. We would build a fire in the Franklin stove and cook our dinner over the flames. Mom got quite creative at the meals we ate those nights; she started with standard camping fare, but eventually let her creativity take over and we made all sorts of wonderful things. We read by candlelight, did our homework, and then played board games as a family. My brother and I even had special toys we only got to play with on the 'no electricity nights.' I don't remember what his was, but mine was this amazing book of paper dolls with costumes to dress them up as different characters from books. One of the set of costumes was from Shakespeare's *Romeo and Juliet*. I made my dad tell me the story, and I fell in love with Shakespeare that night . . . perhaps leading to my ultimate career choice as a literature teacher. I have continued this tradition with my children, even though it wasn't for the same reasons as my parents. They love the family time just as much as my brother and I always did, and it helps us find time to just be together without the disruptions of modern life."

My boyfriend is Russian. He darns his socks. Let me say that again. *He darns his socks.* Who sews socks anymore? You throw them out when they get holes and you buy new ones at Wal-Mart. Remember when we used to take appliances to a repair shop because it was cheaper than buying a new one? I'm barely old enough to remember it myself.

Russians, as a group, hate waste. They seem offended by the concept of paper towels. You wipe up some water and throw it away? Theirs is not a cerebral concern about "the environment"—they don't want to spend money on something you're just going to toss out. They are still operating under the notion that thrift is good, a notion we've moved steadily away from, with an accelerating pace since the 1950s.

When an American decides to try something new, for example learning to make sushi, the first thing she is likely to do is go to the store and buy the right equipment—a six-piece Japanese bowl set, a wooden sushi boat, a sesame seed toaster, and wooden chopsticks. In fact, the American might become so enamored with shopping for sushi stuff that she completely fails to get around to making sushi.

Faced with the same urge to make sushi, a Russian will look around her kitchen and see what she can use. A Russian bowl is as good as a Japanese bowl. A pan is a sesame toaster. Russians are like flight controller Gene Krantz in the movie *Apollo 13* (I told you I love this movie). He said, "I don't care about what anything was designed to do, I care about what it *can* do."

Everything in a Russian kitchen is a tool. In the American kitchen, complete with yogurt makers and electric omelet pans and George Foreman grills, the would-be sushi chef is stymied. It is as if having a perfect tool for each task has made our imaginations atrophy; our creative mind becomes a vestigial organ like the appendix.

Aren't you just a little too clever to put your gray matter on snooze control? Haven't you always wanted to try gardening, sewing, woodwork? Here's your chance. Nothing increases your confidence like realizing you can make your own table lamp from construction-site scraps. You might just start thinking of yourself as a craftsperson. That's a much better category for yourself than "lazy bum."

One note of caution: Books on thrift love to go on and on about crafts. If you're into it, crafting can be a fun, creative hobby. On the other hand, be skeptical about the claims of great financial savings. Buying tools at a craft store like Michael's can cost more than buying the thing pre-made at a Wal-Mart or thrift shop. For example, you can always find nice candles at the dollar store, but a candle-making kit at the craft store could set you back $22. There are benefits to crafting, of course, but unless you enjoy it, don't think that making your own oven mitts will pull you out of poverty. Crafting is best when you are able to repurpose items you already have.

> **Factoid:** Asphalt now covers 2 percent of the entire country, as well as 50 percent of many metropolitan areas.

19

How to Eat II: Dumpster Diving

··

"A pilaf builds instinctively, naturally. Talking about food for the revolution, the fight and after, may seem irrelevant to some who have not yet considered how the people will be fed or how they themselves will eat."

—ITA JONES, *THE GRUBBAG, AN UNDERGROUND COOKBOOK*, 1971

Here is something to be thankful for: you do not live downwind of the property of David Dickinson, the owner and manager of Midwest Feeding Company. His neighbors may have settled in Nebraska for the clean air and lack of industrial smog. They probably never imagined they'd have to face a two-thousand-ton pile of burning cow shit.

If you're not from farm country, you may not have heard about manure fires or, for that matter, thought much about the quantity of manure those big factory farms produce. Dickinson's feedlot, about twenty miles west of Lincoln, takes in as many as 12,000 cows at a time from ranchers and fattens them for market. If you fatten cows, they produce a lot of manure—a pile 100 feet long, 30 feet high, and 50 feet wide to be precise. As the dung mountain slowly decomposes, it produces heat. *The Lincoln Journal Star* dryly observed: "The combustible nature of ruminant manure has been common knowledge for centuries."

Dickinson's cow patty combustion was especially dramatic. It simmered for four months. Fire fighters who were called in to douse the bovine byproduct blaze described the smell as "your worst nightmare." So imagine owning a restaurant a mile and a half downwind. Enormous piles of poo are only one of the unfortunate side effects of our modern system of factory farms.

Of course, the current system of food production has created numerous benefits: unlimited food, unlimited variety, and endless choices. Go to the grocery store and you will not only find cereal, you'll find wheat cereal, rice cereal, and corn cereal. You will not only find raisin bran, you'll find six brands of raisin bran. You can buy the fresh-squeezed organic fruit drinks in the plastic bottles at the front of the store with the produce or find juice in large aluminum cans in the center or go to the frozen food aisle and get the little tubes of orange juice concentrate. A typical American supermarket carries more than 25,000 items on its shelves. We have access to more than 1,000 types of shampoo and more than 2,000 skin care products.

All of this abundance has its price—and that is waste. Almost inconceivable waste occurs at nearly every link in our food chain. Not only are there burning cow manure pits out west, Dumpsters full of perfectly edible food stuffs are carted away from our restaurants and grocery stores every day, even as you try to figure out how to get yourself fed with only $2.37 left in your checking account. This is where "freeganism" comes in. Freegans believe in "limited participation in the conventional economy and minimal consumption of resources." That means salvaging things that would otherwise end up in landfills.

Shy about diving into a trash dumpster to find treasures? There is no reason to feel that way any more. Here's how you explain it: You have not been reduced to picking through garbage to feed yourself. You have been elevated to a political and socially savvy lifestyle that aims to save the world from its excesses. You are not picking through the trash, you are liberating waste.

"The solution to world hunger can be found in the waste bins of the United States," Freegan Adam Weissman told a Boston TV station.

Americans dump 38 million tons of food each year, according to the Environmental Protection Agency. Restaurants and supermarkets discard about $30 billion worth of food each year. Just 5 percent of our leftovers could feed four million people for one day. Disposing of food waste costs $1 billion a year. The United Nations says our leftovers could satisfy every single empty stomach in Africa. It's not just the United States. France's food wastes could feed the Democratic Republic of Congo and Italy's could feed the hungry of Ethiopia. The UK and Japan discard between 30 and 40 percent of their food produce each year.

The food that rots in landfills releases methane, a more potent greenhouse gas than CO_2. The UK's Waste and Resources Action Program estimates that if we stopped throwing out edible food, the impact on CO_2 emissions would be the equivalent of taking 1 in 5 cars off the road.

If you don't find the solution to world hunger in that dumpster, at least you can find the solution to your own. Tired of boxed macaroni and cheese, Spam, and ramen noodles? A well-considered trash run could raise your standard of living. Head to the dumpster of one of those upscale grocery stores, a health food store, or an ethnic market. You just might find discarded caviar, as Ryan Beiler, an editor and Freegan, did.

"On my very first dumpster run, I went into Homer Simpson–drool mode at finding several pounds of smoked salmon—a delicacy I could never justify buying in real life," Beiler wrote.

Back in your student days, you probably furnished your dorm with furniture people left by the curb to be hauled away, right? So why not fill your kitchen the same way now. The first big Dumpster discovery can usually take away the squeamishness of rummaging through society's castoffs. Michael, a North Carolinian who blogs about his freegan adventures at freejunkfood.blogspot.com has found endless foodstuffs as well as other desirable objects: Lindor truffles, disposable cameras, a cordless shaver, a Microsoft keyboard, and a 3 GB flash drive.

"I have been checking pharmacies lately and have found that they have almost as much valuable stuff in their trash as any grocery store," Michael blogged. "It makes me wonder what other kinds of stores have great dumps that I have not considered yet."

Most of the articles that have been published on freegans point out that they are mostly upper middle class and do not need to dig through the trash. (Apparently it is socially acceptable to liberate waste, as long as you don't actually need it.) *The Los Angeles Times*, for example, featured a woman who once spent $100,000 a year on fancy clothes, food, and the mortgage on a two-bedroom co-op in Greenwich Village. She now has embraced the freegan lifestyle and forages for groceries, garnishes her salad with weeds picked from neighbors' yards, and freezes her surplus food finds. She sold her co-op and now bikes to work from a one-bedroom apartment. Her annual expenditures now are $25,000 a year. Being a Freegan is a hip thing to do.

Factoid: The average American throws out 4.6 pounds of garbage a day. Americans throw away 470 pounds of food a year—the estimated value of this food is $590 (per household). About 14 percent of food brought into an American house is thrown out, and 15 percent of discarded food is thrown away unopened.

Dumpster divers relish the thrill of the hunt. You never know what you are going to find. Researchers from The Garbage Project, a group that performs archeological anaylsis of municipal solid waste, once discovered a diamond ring amid a mass of potato peels.

Trash haulers themselves are well ahead of the game when it comes to liberating waste. For years they have rescued treasures before tossing them into the backs of their trucks. Bobby Williams, who manages the family trash collection business in Ft. Washington, Maryland, organized his team for a major recycling effort. He gives his employees a list of desirable items such as bicycles, toys, small appliances, and furniture. The waste haulers divert them before they get into the waste stream, and Williams takes them home and repairs them. His wife removes spots on upholstery and sprays disinfectant on toys. When their garage is full, they load up a truck with the perfectly usable stuff and donate it to neighborhood non-profits.

Artists also take advantage of the waste stream. In Philadelphia, a group called the Dumpster Divers takes society's dregs and transforms them into art. The group's motto is Ejectamentum Nummi Nostrum— "Your trash is our cash."

"I believe trash is simply a failure of imagination," writes Philadelphia Dumpster Diver Neil Benson. "Creative re-use of objects is re-vitalization: Things are born again—it is spiritually fulfilling to turn trash into treasure. It is artistic alchemy with the artist as wizard."

If you are planning to go trash scavenging for the first time, there are a few things you should remember. First, there is some risk involved. Not so much from rotted food—most food is so thoroughly wrapped in plastic these days that it would take a great effort to permeate it with filth, and sell-by dates are not actually "expiration dates"—but from the other garbage and the dumpster itself. "Solid waste hauler" ranks third on the list of the deadliest jobs in the United States. Some of those injuries happen back at the plant, where workers are mauled by compacting equipment, but you will face some of the dangers they face if you enter their environment. Garbage men are sometimes cut by broken jars and discarded hypodermic needles. They have to deal with the raccoons and snakes that get into the cans in search of yummy food scraps. Even worse, trash collectors have to deal with impatient drivers who try to pass stopped garbage trucks and run over their operators in the process. Someone could sideswipe you as you emerge from a dumpster in the dark.

Now that you've been warned, here are some expert tips on dumpster diving technique from the folks at freegan.info. If you're looking for fun, free things to do with your friends, a freegan forage may fit the bill. It is always best to go with friends. This way, one person gets to jump right in to the dumpster, while another stays outside to take the booty. Needless to say, you'll want to wear comfortable clothes that you don't mind getting dirty. The best time to search dumpsters unmolested is late at night or very early in the morning, but even if you go during the day, it's going to be dark inside the dumpster, so you'll need some kind of light. A flashlight will do, but a headlight or a lantern that you can set down works even better because it keeps your hands free. I shouldn't have to tell you this, but don't jump into a trash compactor.

Be discriminating about waste food. If you're not sure it is fresh or edible or tasty, leave it where it is. You may find fish that was discarded before its sell-by date. That's great, but do you know how long it was sitting in the dumpster and at what temperature? Champion Dumpster Divers say that bread is always plentiful and that donut shop dumpsters are nearly always full of two-day-old sweets, but restaurants will yield you little more than a mélange of table scraps and potato peelings. Potato peelings, incidentally, are the largest category of food waste in household garbage, according to The Garbage Project. They account for 7 percent by weight of the food material we throw out. In all, edible and inedible food debris accounts for about a fifth of household garbage.

Diving etiquette: Re-close any bags that you opened and never leave trash strewn about. It is not considerate of the businesses, who are responsible for keeping that area tidy. If they get annoyed enough, they will lock up their garbage and you will lose your gold mine.

20

Identical Strangers:*
The World of Work

"You are married to a career, and why some people marry what they don't love is beyond me."

—ALBERT LEE, U.S. AUTHOR AND SPEECHWRITER

There is a Cincinnati-based company that provides work clothes to businesses. Its trucks and billboards are emblazoned with the slogan "The Uniform People." Whenever I see one of their vans, nightmare images of Stepford factories spring to mind. I see an assembly line peopled by identical strangers, performing the same tasks, in the same clothing, with the same Father-Knows-Best expressions on their matching faces. In my mind they are usually in black and white.

And here is the big problem with a lot of what passes for work today. We feel like the uniform people of my daydreams, pounded into round holes whether or not we are square, round, or oblong.

The philosopher Ernest van den Haag put it this way, "The benefits of mass production are reaped only by matching de-individualizing work with equally de-individualizing consumption. Failure to repress

---

* When I dreamed of being a rock star in seventh grade, "The Identical Strangers" was the name I planned to give my band. I still think I should have been a rock star, but my career ambitions were unfairly thwarted by the fact that I never actually learned to play an instrument.

individual personality in or after working hours is costly; in the end, the production of standardized things by persons also demands the production of standardized persons." The uniform people.

If you've been on a job hunt lately, you know that the interviewers view you not as a complex spiritual being with hopes and aspirations but as a receptacle for a collection of skills that can be matched to a preexisting job slot. The lower the job pays, the more testing they seem to do, with long and often unintentionally humorous quizzes designed to determine if you are likely to steal or if you might get the company involved in a sexual harassment lawsuit. If you want the job, when they ask if you would return an extra $5 given to you with your change, be sure to give the fairly obvious answer they're looking for regardless of what actually comes to your mind. And remember to smile and look pleasant as they hand you the cup for your urine sample and check off the box that says you give them permission to check your credit report (with any luck they won't actually do it).

Once an employer hires you, they know it can be very hard to fire you. You might sue for wrongful termination. Employers have also on occasion found themselves embroiled in expensive "negligent hiring" lawsuits. They're damned if they do, and damned if they don't. They need to have at least a pseudo-scientific hiring method and a paper trail that explains why they chose you, just in case you turn out to be a secret ax murderer. The difficulty is that they have become so worried about not making mistakes that they have stopped really evaluating the candidates they encounter.

You may think, for example, that the employer really wants to know what you think when they hand you a piece of plain, unruled paper and ask you to write out your goals for the next five years. But they're not actually going to read about your quest to become an organizational leader—they're going to perform handwriting analysis to see if you're a team player.

This hard data approach finds reasons to exclude rather than to include a new hire. You may have a sense of your potential, but your would-be employer is only concerned with your past. Yet psychological studies prove that people are happiest and most creative when they feel they are making progress and growing. Most work environments, however, are not able to risk putting an untested person into a position. You may be positive you would be great at a job for which you have no experience, but it will be more than a challenge for you to snag it if anyone comes along who has worked a similar job. After many years on the job, a lot of people feel stuck. They may not feel as if they're learning anything new, but they have racked up too much experience in one area to go back and start from scratch in a new direction.

Ironically, as much as we fret over not being able to demonstrate our potential, getting a promotion often makes things worse, not better. Researcher George Homans found that when a worker gets the keys to the executive washroom, he feels less, not more, satisfied. Getting "Level B" clearance just makes him wonder why he hasn't yet become a "Level A."

Because so much modern work sucks, it fools us into believing we don't like to work. This is unfortunate, because studies show that people report themselves as happiest when they are working toward a goal in a state of flow. We love to work! Yet when you ask that same person if she would be happier working or lounging on a beach, she will invariably tell you to hand over the suntan lotion. We know ourselves that poorly. We have no problem with working. What we don't like is *meaningless* work that makes us a cog in the machinery. What we don't like is feeling we have no direct control over our work lives.

Unfortunately in the age of mega-corporations and economies of scale (aren't all economies of some scale?) more and more people are working for organizations that are too large to make everyone feel like a part of the process. Although most Americans prefer to think of themselves as "middle class," if you define "working class" in terms of power—not having power over when and how you work—then it has been estimated a good 60 percent of us are "working class."

As someone who grew up in Detroit in the shadow of GM, Ford, and Chrysler, I have known more than my fair share of automotive company employees. Not one of them knows how to fix a car. If we can't feel entirely connected to the end goal, at least we can share in the profits, but that is rarely ever enough to create a feeling of true satisfaction.

In an interview with Linda Montano, author of *Performance Artists Talking in the Eighties*, musician Robert Ashley discussed how he learned about job satisfaction watching a documentary on the building of the Panama Canal. The Panamanians who worked on the project didn't know anything about money.

"... so what they enjoyed about the piece was not making money that they could spend but that somebody came along and organized and presented to these people this huge-scale project and social interaction," Ashley says. "... These men were working like maniacs, because they were having fun, not because they were being paid. And the guys who came from America thought, 'This is wonderful, we don't have to pay them.' As soon as the piece was over, the people who worked on the canal kept wanting to have another party. They wanted to build another Panama Canal, and they were sad, not because they didn't have any money but because there was nothing like that in the future for them."

So what I am saying here is that if you thought you could assume a "broke is beautiful" identity so that you can swing on a hammock all day, I'm sorry to have to disabuse you of this notion. A truly satisfying pauper's life is not the life of leisure, but a life spent working with complete abandon on something that is in line with your dreams and values. "Broke and Beautiful" means being cash-poor and work-rich. If you are broke because you'd rather lie around with your feet up than put in an honest day's labor, well, you're just lazy. (But see the next chapter for some tips on being a slacker anyway.)

"Hail Mary. Got to Race."

Bishop Willie Walsh warned readers of *The Mirror* that one group of workers was suffering from extreme overwork and that they were starting to experience burnout. "People don't appreciate the amount of work priests do," he said. "Priests do more work than the vast majority of people I know." Priests are having to carry a heavier load, he said, because of a continuing decline in numbers of clergy.

THINGS TO BE THANKFUL FOR

THE BAD DAYS AT WORK EDITION

Did your boss do his best Donald Trump impersonation and then have someone watch while you put the picture of your kids in a box and walked it to your car? Then you may be one of the thousands of Americans who lost their jobs last month. (The number of people who get to make millions by firing people on their own reality TV shows? One.)

Yes, it's humiliating to be stripped of your ID badge and men's room key. Your boss may have called security, but I'm guessing he didn't torch your desk. This is more than can be said for one of National Cash Register founder John Henry Patterson's employees. Patterson took "firing" literally. One executive returned from a business trip to find that his desk had been hauled out to the lawn, doused in kerosene, and set ablaze. Patterson once axed his entire accounting department by marching them down to the company boiler room and ordering them to toss their ledgers into the fire.

———————◆———————

There are just so many new and creative ways a work day can suck. You'll be delighted to know your boss has not thought of all of them. Before we get into individual achievements in horrible work environments and the prizes for the worst ever employers, let's talk about bad careers in general. Let me start by saying that in 2000 I wrote a book called *The Pocket Encyclopedia of Aggrava-*

tion, and in it I included what I thought had to be one of the worst jobs out there:

> Many medical schools now offer genital teaching associate programs to show students how to make patients more comfortable during the less modest exams. Surrogate patients can undergo 10–20 prostate, hernia, rectal, breast, or pelvic exams by medical students in a single day. The University of South Florida pays the subjects $37.50 an hour, in case you wanted to apply.

The punch line is that as soon as the book came out I received e-mail from people asking how to get this job. Shows how much I know about attractive careers.

I'm betting though that I won't get too many requests for referrals on Alan Lefler's job. Alan, of Des Moines, Iowa, worked for the Scott County Humane Society. His job was to burn the carcasses of the euthanized dogs and cats. Seeing Fluffy and Fido going up in flames day after day gave him nightmares and insomnia. The odor often made him vomit and the smoke made him physically ill. When he filed for unemployment benefits he listed his reasons for leaving as the "constant stoking, tending, poking, and prodding of the burning carcasses, suffering the stench and odor and actually seeing the flames consume the body." The job paid $10,600 a year. Sounds like there's a vacancy there if you want it.

Popular Science magazine publishes an annual list of the worst jobs in science. Among its suggestions are "anal-wart researcher," "worm parasitologist," and "tampon squeezer." That last one was for a study of vaginal yeast infections.

A late nineteenth-century San Francisco character, Leonard Borchardt, who went by the professional name "Oofty Goofty—The Wild Man of Borneo" hated traditional jobs. He tried a number of stunts, including an attempt at pushing a wheelbarrow from San Francisco to New York (he didn't get far) before stumbling onto his true calling—human punching bag. A small, skinny man, he claimed to have an exceptionally strong skull. He charged ten cents for a kicking, twenty five cents for a caning, and fifty cents to be beaten with a baseball bat. For a time he made a painful but lucrative living. That is until the famous boxer John L. Sullivan paid him fifty cents to pound him with a billiard cue and broke it in three places. Oofty decided to retire after that one.

In 2004, a Tokyo electrical contractor, whose company went bankrupt, decided to take the Oofty Goofty approach to riches. He walked around his city with a pair of boxing gloves and offered passersby the opportunity to take swings at him for the equivalent of $9 a minute. He encouraged his attackers to further relieve stress by shouting at him as they swang. He told the *Los Angeles Times* that he brought in about $200 a night.

21

Alternative Identity: Downshifters, Voluntary Simplicity, and Slackers

....

"Men, for the sake of getting a living, forget to live."

**—MARGARET FULLER, US AUTHOR AND
WOMEN'S RIGHTS ACTIVIST**

I recently found myself outside an IMAX theater advertising what it called "A 4-D" movie. Since the fourth dimension is time, it was a clever, if meaningless way to add some excitement to a movie poster. *Every film* exists in the dimension of time.

But imagine a time before time. That is to say, a time before time was measured, quantified, put in little boxes. Some time around 1335 someone invented a mechanical device to click out the seconds, minutes, and hours. If you worked in an office cubicle in 1334 and you came in to work to hear your boss shout, "You're late!" You would reply, "What is *late*?"

In those days, people measured the passage of time by the rising and setting of the sun and by the falling leaves, freezing lakes, and the return of the migrating birds. Time, in the medieval sense, connected humans to nature.

As we shifted to measuring ever smaller units of time on machines, we began to organize our lives to their pace and rhythm. Ninety years without slumbering, tick-tock, tick-tock, our life seconds numbering, tick-tock tick-tock.

Can you even imagine a world in which alarm clocks simply do not exist? This was the state of things as late as 1875. A year later, the windup alarm clock hit the market. The phrase, "Sorry, I overslept!" entered our vocabulary shortly thereafter. Factory punch clocks were the next innovation. They appeared a few years later.

"The clock is the operating system of modern capitalism," wrote Carl Honoré, author of *In Praise of Slowness*, "the thing that makes everything else possible—meetings, deadlines, contracts, manufacturing processes, schedules, transport, working shifts."

Until the early 1880s, when railroads began to connect geographically diverse populations at high speed, there was no reason to coordinate time. For example, New Orleans kept its own pace (it still does, just not with the clock) and was twenty-three minutes behind Baton Rouge, only eighty miles west. This made it mind-bogglingly inefficient to conduct business with people in different parts of the nation or the world.

By 1855, most of Britain was accepting the time transmitted from the Royal Observatory in Greenwich. In 1884, twenty-seven nations agreed to a standard system of time zones based on Greenwich as the prime meridian. By 1911, most of the world was in temporal synch.

Around this time we started to become obsessed with "deadlines." The word "deadline" has its origin in Civil War prison camps. Towards the end of the war, as prison populations grew, and wire for perimeter fences became scarce, authorities planted markers and painted a line between them. Anyone seen crossing the line would be summarily shot. (They apparently had no scarcity of bullets.) Eventually, the concept of a line of death that must not be crossed came into newspaper parlance as a time limit that can not be exceeded, and from there it became part of our common vocabulary.

There are still cultures in the world that view time more holistically, as a cycle rather than a straight line made up of small units. French filmmaker Richard Martin Jordan visited the small island of Tanna, which is home to one of the last remaining "Cargo Cults" to make the film *Dieu est Americain*. Such cults sprang up throughout the Pacific Islands during World War II when American soldiers with ships full of more material wealth than the natives had seen in a lifetime arrived on their shores. On Tanna, practitioners of this faith worship a mythical pilot, John Frum, and hold the U.S. flag as sacred. The islanders speak a pidgin mix of Melanesian—English-French—to communicate. "Titi belong basket" means "bra," for example. In interviews in the film, religious leader Isaac the One's Ipeukel dialect is dotted with such expressions as "three days," "six o'clock," and "every time." It becomes clear that every word related to time is borrowed from English, implying that the native language had little use for such expressions prior to the arrival of the Americans.

"Isaac and his men spend their time doing nothing," Jordan said. "Their relation to time doesn't have anything to do with ours. We have everything except time."

Isaac told Jordan that his people were "the opposite" of the Europeans. "We are poor, you are rich," he said, "We have time, you lack it, we don't work, you work all your life! We eat what we plant, you don't touch the earth any more, you don't caress the trees, you don't look up at the sky anymore! . . . You're just curious, rich and idle."

When you work for someone, you are exchanging your time for money. They pay you, and you donate a percentage of your life's energy—a percentage of your life—to their cause. We never seem to feel overappreciated and underwhelmed. It can be hard to get sympathy when you're overworked and stretched to the limit. When you complain to someone that you're working two jobs, and you're chasing the kids and you're tired, instead of "Gee, that's terrible," you usually hear, "Me too, and I have my night classes and this report to finish . . ." That's because just about everybody feels she has too much on her plate.

Pam Ryan and Denise Koufogiannakis, two Canadian librarians, wrote about the "culture of busy" that permeates their field in a professional journal (frenzied Canadian librarians—who knew?). "Librarians engage in this battle for superiority, based not on individual accomplishments—we're far too modest for that—but rather on one's 'volume of busy,'" they wrote. "The point of this battle is to prove that we do more and have less free time than our peers, and are thus more important. We have so much on our plates, we cannot possibly take on another thing, so we are increasingly forgiven from additional contribution by nature of our busy excellence."

This would be fine, I guess, if we took out our frustration on our bosses. But the people who suffer the most from our inattention and stress are the people closest to us. Researcher Ellen Galinsky recently asked 1,000 kids from a variety of backgrounds to identify what they most needed from their parents. What they rated as most important was "being there for me." When asked if they could have one wish, the children said they wished that their parents were less tired and stressed. There is a vast difference, you see, between going somewhere and GO-GO-Going!

Once I was in a train station, and I overheard a woman asking a little boy what he wanted to be when he grew up. Anyway, this boy was about kindergarten age. He looked up at his grandmother and said that when he grew up he wanted to be a "vacation guy."

The woman asked him what that was. She must have thought he wanted to be a travel agent, or a tour group leader. But no, he explained that a "vacation guy" is someone who goes on vacation and then comes home and watches TV.

Unfortunately, they walked off before I could go up and ask the boy where I go to get that job.

Downshifters and practitioners of voluntary simplicity are taking their best stab at it. They are folks who think time is more valuable than money, that the true measure of wealth is their ability to be present for the people they love, and they make their career choices accordingly.

As the cost of living goes up in cities, they move into the "exurbs"— small towns and communities out of commuting range of the major metros. They may embrace "slow food"—planting a garden, cooking from scratch, baking bread, learning to appreciate fine wine, mixing cocktails. As a downshifter, you can take a long nap. Who knows how many of our social ills can be attributed to the fact that we don't have time for a nap in the afternoon like they do in South America?

When you're over extended, you're simply not available to life. "The symptoms of *laziness* and of physical and mental *burnout* are pretty much the same," said productivity author and speaker Laura Stack. "You can't motivate yourself to do anything. I haven't commissioned a scientific study on this, but I would guess that a good 95 percent of the time when we kick ourselves for being too lazy, we're really just tired."

According to creativity researcher Teresa Amabile of the Harvard Business School, people are least creative when they are fighting the clock. As a matter of fact, Amabile discovered what she calls a "time-pressure hangover." Not only is creativity suppressed when people are working under a deadline, they continue to come up with fewer imaginative solutions over the next two days. Down time is a necessary part of the creative process. (See the chapter on daydreaming for more on this.)

You should know, too, that "the hectic pace of modern life" has been something people have complained about for a long time. "It is an age of nervousness . . . the growing malady of the day, the physiological feature of the age," said a *New York Tribune* editorial. "Nowhere are the rush and hurry and overstrain of life more marked than in this much-achieving Nation. . . . Inventions, discoveries, achievements of science all add to the sum of that which is to be learned, and widen the field in which there is work to be done. If knowledge has increased, we should take more time for acquiring it. . . . For it would be a sorry ending of this splendid age of learning and of labor to be known as an age of unsettled brains and shattered nerves." The article was written in 1895.

So you're stressed, I'm stressed, we're all stressed, and we've probably always been stressed. You want off this crazy thing? Define yourself as a downshifter. You are not someone who is not getting promoted, but someone promoting a more authentic lifestyle. The down-shifter persona is a great one for the recently laid off. "I may be broke, but at least I'm not running myself ragged any more. I've started to read *Remembrance of Things Past*."

The award for the most surprising downshifter must go to Dee Hock, inventor of the Visa card. Hock is an idealist who believed his credit card creation would allow "spontaneous interconnection into an equitable, enduring, twenty-first-century society in harmony with the human spirit and the biosphere."

It didn't, and Hock, who never liked to be shackled by bureaucracy, left Bank of America and now lives on a small farm in Northern California where James Scurlock, author of *Maxed Out*, reports that he spends his time "tilling the soil, discussing philosophy with his tractor (which he has named 'Thee Ancient One'), and his subconscious (which he has named 'Old Money Mind.')"

Technically, to be a "downshifter" rather than a simple practitioner of voluntary simplicity, you're supposed to have had a well-paying job in the past. The downshifter has gotten the religion; a practitioner of voluntary simplicity may have always had the religion. In fact, as with the Mennonites and Quakers, this life style often has a spiritual component. You are not merely simplifying life to make it more pleasurable for you, but so that you can use your surplus to perform good works for others. You conserve so that you can serve.

A perfect example is that of the family, quoted in Mennonite author Doris Janzen Longacre's *Living More with Less*, who returned from a stint living in Haiti as medical doctors in a home with no electricity plumbing, or running water. When they returned to the United States, they called the local welfare department to find out the allotment for a family of five in food and clothing and used that as their budget—a level of thrift that ensured their empathy for the poorest among us.

The downshift narrative, on the other hand, is a different take on the American Dream. It goes like this: "I was making $250,000 as a computer engineer. Then I realized there was much more to life than money."

But don't let your missing quarter mil leave you out. You too can have a conversion from the pursuit of status to the pursuit of happiness. Any job where you were unappreciated and run ragged will serve the narrative, and haven't we all had those?

On the other hand, if you have never worn a tie, you listen to alternative music, and you like to watch subtitled foreign films in the dark to ripen the depression, you may want to cultivate a more hipster variant of the downshifter's life, the slacker.

Slackers had their big moment of fame in the 1990s when they were the subjects of movies like *Slackers, Clerks, Reality Bites,* and *Office Space.* But they carry on a long and proud tradition of alienated young people (usually, it must be said, from comfortable middle-class backgrounds). Before slacker cool there were the hippies, and before that the beats. The term *beatnik* was coined by Herb Caen, a columnist for the *San Francisco Chronicle*, in 1958. He described a party hosted by *Look Magazine* for fifty beatniks, "Over 250 bearded cats and kits were on hand, slopping up Mike Cowles's free booze. They're only Beat, you know, when it comes to work."

Finding slacker role models can be a challenge. As Tom Luntz, author of *Doing Nothing*, pointed out, "Anti-work attitudes are unreliable. . . . The famous or almost famous idlers, loafers, loungers, and slackers throughout history had to produce work about not working in order for us to know them. And many of them, it turns out, were closet workaholics. . . . Real slackers would be, logically, too slack to write their own history."

Of course, that depends a lot on the definition of *work*. The group CLAWS, or "Creating Livable Alternatives to Wage Slavery" (their URL is whywork.org), posits the theory that there is a vast difference between jobs and work. "We can define work simply as *the expenditure of energy in a productive process,* and leisure as the expenditure of energy *without* productive result," they explain, "We're not saying one is good and the other bad—they're just two ways of being. We are not against being productive, and we recognize the satisfaction that can result from being engaged in productive activity of one's own choosing." In other words, there's nothing wrong with work, per se, as long as you chose to do it yourself.

Being a slacker or a modern-day beatnik is not as socially acceptable as being a downshifter, and why should it be? A big part of this identity is thumbing your nose at the establishment. You can't expect the establishment to send you love letters in return. The other downside is that unless you have an ironic sense of outsider cool, it's just not going to work for you. But if you're young, you like to wear black, and you firmly believe that leisure is the natural state of being, then this may be just the option for you.

Are You a Serf?

During the Middle Ages, when there was no concept of social advancement, people worked to meet their basic needs and to fulfill their expected roles in society. Religious celebration was a vital part of life, and people did no labor on about 150 holy days. These days, in the United States, most working people get only one week off beyond weekends and a two-week vacation. That adds up to about 111 days of rest per year. So peasants in the Middle Ages had more time off work than we do today.

Acting Your Age

"The trouble with growing older is that it gets progressively tougher to find a famous historical figure who didn't amount to much when he was your age."

—BILL VAUGHAN, U.S. COLUMNIST AND AUTHOR

You don't have to look far to find someone who is broke and savoring the joy of life. Just peer into your own past. Remember when you were in college and you found some bricks and boards in a dumpster and made your own bookshelves? Or that time your boyfriend—now your husband—couldn't afford to take you out so he planned a romantic dinner at his place. It was macaroni and cheese and a box o' wine drunk out of unmatched plastic cups and was probably the best date you've ever had.

Before my junior year as a college theater student, I had the opportunity to work for an entire summer with an improvisational theater troupe at an amusement park. It sounded like a better job than delivering pizza, so I embarked on a path that would eventually add "professional mime" to my resume.

I imagine someone did a poll before the 1989 season at Dorney Park and Wildwater Kingdom. The poll must have asked park patrons what they liked and disliked about their Dorney experience. They said they liked fast roller-coasters, water slides, and wave pools but that they got bored waiting in the lines. This could be a big problem, the park administrators reasoned, since they were about to unveil Hercules, the tallest wooden roller coaster in the world.

The solution? Roving entertainers! "You'll meet these strolling entertainers all through the park!," a Dorney brochure boasted. "Magicians, musicians, mimes, and more!" I was part of the "more."

The larger troupe of roving entertainers consisted of a female mime, a magician, various jugglers, unicycle riders, balloon animal makers, and a trombone player. The entertainment company that hired us also provided a host and dancers for a theatrical game show called Dorney Duels. Imagine *Family Feud* with a comic host in a gold lamé jacket and three beautiful women dancing and singing in glittery dresses. The stagefolk and roving performers were all housed in barely furnished apartments (they listed smoke detectors as a selling point in their brochure). My comedy partner and I roomed with a mime, a statuesque, blonde Ohioan whose hobbies included singing, Ouija, and channeling a spirit guide. We decorated our walls with slips of paper on which we'd written favorite quotes and pictures drawn by various entertainer friends. Our rent and utilities were paid for by the company. Perhaps to conserve electricity, the apartments did not have televisions. We didn't miss them. We entertained ourselves after work by playing improvisational theater games. We had a lot of parties. After a particularly rowdy night, you'd wake up to find the place littered with balloon animals. We usually kept our doors open and shouted to our fellow actors who lived across the hall. They liked to stay up late doing drum circles. That is, until the people in the apartment next to us called the police to make them stop.

As you can imagine, I felt anything but poor in these surroundings, even though the furnishings were as Spartan as you can imagine. Your history may contain fewer balloon animals, but I am willing to bet you have similar memories—where the lack of money only contributed to the charm of the moment.

Yet if you were to try to replicate that lifestyle today—to furnish your home entirely with cast-off milk cartons, or invite your date to sit with you in the library or split a cheeseburger at McDonald's—it wouldn't seem charming at all. It would seem, to put it bluntly, age inappropriate. What was a lark at twenty seems kind of pathetic now that you're thirty or forty. Why should that be?

To everything, turn, turn, turn. . . . There is a time at which we deem it appropriate to "find yourself" and a time at which we generally agree you should have found yourself. We imagine ourselves traveling along a yard stick that is divided into years instead of inches. There are deadlines by which we expect certain levels of success, and since it is much more difficult to judge your "arrival" in terms of subjective experience, we look for outward signs like having a house, a car, or a job title. It may seem as though these are your personal goals and deadlines, but they are almost entirely created by one thing—peer pressure.

If you thought peer pressure was something you gave into at twelve and now you've matured and moved on, think again. We just call it by different names: social standing, image, reputation. The drive to maintain a good social standing seems to be hard-wired into our brains.

Scientists at the National Institute of Mental Health and Japan's National Institute for Physiological Sciences used different methods in separate studies and came up with the same results. We process social standing and monetary rewards in the same part of the brain, the striatum, which may explain something about our tendency to equate the two.

"Although we intuitively know that a good reputation makes us feel good, the idea that a good reputation is a reward had long been just an assumption without scientific proof," researcher Norihiro Sadato told *Scientific American.*

As social beings we create social norms, and we're hardly even aware of them or their force. We internalize the values so completely that we think of certain life events as "signs of maturity" rather than "socially normative behaviors."

You've probably never been told this, or seen it written out this way, but here are the rules as to the appropriate ages for particular life activities:

Time for a man to marry: 20–25

Time for a woman to marry: 19–24

Time to be done with your schooling and go to work: 20–22

Time when men should be settled on their career: 24–25

Time when a man has the most responsibilities: 35–50

Time when a man accomplishes the most: 40–50

That is the result of a survey of middle class people, aged 40–70, and published as part of the the study "Age Norms, Age Constraints and Adult Socialization" in the book *Middle Age and Aging* compiled by Bernice Levin Neugarten. "When the behavior occurs outside that span of years, it is regarded as inappropriate and is negatively sanctioned," the author wrote.

What if you happen to have "missed" one of these cultural deadlines? Think of Malaysian men's genitals. Steve J. Ayan and Iris Tatjana Calliess, in the *Scientific American* article "Abnormal as Norm," use the example of men in Malaysia who believe they have a condition called "koro" to illustrate how different cultures treat varied behaviors as normal. Men who think they have koro are afraid their genitals will retract into their bodies. So to prevent it, they hang weights on their penises.

"The fear, and the uncomfortable antidote, is not common, yet it is accepted in this long-standing culture," they wrote, "But in a Western country, an adult male who acted on such a belief would certainly be labeled as emotionally disturbed."

If pumping iron with your privates is normal in another part of the world, then surely getting settled into your career at age twenty-five was not carved in stone by God. When you strip all of your cultural conditioning away, what do you think is a better measure of a person's maturity: wisdom or a house with a two-car garage? And a follow-up question: is it wiser to search one's own values to determine what would be a satisfying life or to chase after a particular goal because of a sense that it is socially appropriate to do so?

Remember this advice from Kidshealth.org: "It is tough to be the only one who says 'no' to peer pressure, but you can do it. Paying attention to your own feelings and beliefs about what is right and wrong can help you know the right thing to do. Inner strength and self-confidence can help you stand firm, walk away, and resist doing something when you know better."

"When we think about the past, we focus on our childhoods, to a time when our parents protected us from the world. As adults, even if society's gotten better, the sense of being sheltered is gone. Nobody's taking care of you anymore, so it feels like everything is getting more worrisome, even if objectively everything is getting better."

—CHRISTOPHER JENCKS, HARVARD UNIVERSITY PROFESSOR

23 **Libraries: A Love Story**

....

"In the library I felt better—words you could trust and look at till you understood them, they couldn't change half way through a sentence like people."

—JEANETTE WINTERSON, *ORANGES ARE NOT THE ONLY FRUIT*

Thank God for libraries. Praise be to librarians for making a broke man's life bearable. Glory to the Lord above that the idea of the library was well entrenched in a time of communities and collective works. If the idea were proposed today it would be labeled communist, and Disney would sue to protect its intellectual property from being read without collecting a fee.

Praise be to whatever higher power you believe in that the great thoughts of antiquity, high culture, and modern information are still accessible to anyone with a library card. The American Dream is alive in libraries. The library is an idealistic bow to our value of true meritocracy, knowledge made available to anyone who wants it. No PhD required, no bank account, no credit score, only a curious mind. Glory hallelujah. Hosanna in the highest.

Public libraries, as we know them—where a person of any background can check out all the books he wants for free and take them home—are a distinctly American invention. In old Europe there were manuscript archives, but there was little need for libraries for the masses. The masses could not read to begin with, and there weren't that many books to go around anyway. Until the middle of the fifteenth century, Europe was said to have produced no more than one thousand hand-written books a year.

Medieval archives chained their books to desks like banks do with pens. The idea that you might take a book home to read was impossible. Books, painstakingly reproduced by clerics with quills, were simply too valuable. Checking out a book in those days would be like checking out the *Mona Lisa*.

The printing press, of course, changed things a bit. Books could be copied and copied again by the thousands, and for the first time in history, they were cheap enough to be lendable.

It was that radical Benjamin Franklin who came up with the notion of the lending library. His model was a bit different than the modern library. It was a "social library," which was a kind of book club. (Not the kind that sends you books you don't want if you fail to mail a postcard back.) You paid to join, but then you got to share books with a large group of other people.

Franklin's Library Company, which he referred to as the "public library of Philadelphia," was formed with an idealistic view: to break down class distinctions and allow artisans to become as well-read as the well-born.

"These libraries have improved the general conversation of the Americans, made the common tradesmen and farmers as intelligent as most gentlemen from other countries, and perhaps has contributed in some degree to the stand so generally made throughout the colonies in defense of their privilege," Franklin wrote in his autobiography.

As noble as his sentiment may have been, it would be a while before his concept caught on in a big way. Before 1876, about three thousand social libraries had been founded, mostly in the northeast United States. But they were small and short-lived.

The library movement started to grow as public schools were built across the country. People began to wonder, what good is it to learn *how* to read if you don't have anything *to* read? Legislation in the late-1830s permitted school districts to levy taxes for school libraries. By 1850 Massachusetts had 2,084, while New York schools had some 1.5 million library books.

The patron saint of the American library system was the millionaire Andrew Carnegie. Carnegie poured his fortune into the construction of 1,679 libraries in the United States. The gifts came with the obligation that communities pay for their maintenance and support in perpetuity. Today, more than one thousand of them are still in use as libraries.

"I choose free libraries as the best agencies for improving the masses of the people, because they give nothing for nothing," Carnegie said in 1900. "They only help those who help themselves. They never pauperize. They reach the aspiring, and open to these the chief treasures of the world—those steeped up in books. A taste for reading drives out lower taste."

Interestingly, another great boon to libraries came in the 1950s and '60s, when the nation found itself in a literacy race with the

Soviet Union. The Library Services Act in 1956 and the Library Services and Construction Act of 1964 may have come about in response to a 1950 report, "Public Library Inquiry," published by the Social Science Research Council, which observed that "communist countries have been most active in promoting public library growth within their borders."

Today our nation has ten thousand library systems with 16,500 outlets, and 80 percent are located in rural areas or small towns with fewer than 25,000 people. Modern libraries not only make it possible for the cash-strapped to share in the great literary works of our culture, they provide community programs, lecture series, and playgroups for children. If your Internet access is shut off for nonpayment, don't worry. Head to the library to get online for free. They offer access to licensed databases, homework help, online instruction, access to local community information, and service for job seekers. You can check out movies on DVD. Unlike Blockbuster, they don't claim to charge "no late fees"—you'll have to get them back on time or pay a fine—but they charge no initial fees to borrow a movie. It's hard to beat that. Many libraries likewise lend educational software and video games.

Hoarding is Fundamental

A fifty-eight-year-old New York lawyer was charged with stealing more than fifteen thousand books from the New York Public Library, a hoard discovered by firemen who were checking the building after a fire in another apartment. The books were piled to the ceiling and covered every available inch of floor space. Stolen over a period of ten years, there were so many that it took twenty men three days to move them in seven truckloads. The books were valued at $60,000. The lawyer's only comment outside the courtroom was, "I like to read."

Reasons to Be Glad You Can't Afford a Big Screen TV

"I have two last pieces of advice. First, being pre-approved for a credit card does not mean you have to apply for it. And lastly, the best career advice I can give you is to get your own TV show. It pays well, the hours are good, and you are famous."

**—STEPHEN COLBERT, U.S. COMEDIAN,
COLLEGE COMMENCEMENT**

There is a scene in the psychedelic Monkees movie *Head* in which Peter Tork, trying to shuck off his image as "the dumb one," goes to sit at the foot of a guru in a steam room. (This was before he dressed in a white jump suit and rolled around in a fake head of hair pretending to be dandruff for a television commercial, and after Mickey Dolenz blew up a Coca-Cola machine with a tank.)

Peter, now fully transformed into "the way out one," recounts what he learned to his skeptical band mates: "Psychologically speaking, the human mind, or brain or whatever, is almost incapable of distinguishing between the real and the vividly imagined experience." (Check out a copy of the DVD from your local library to hear the full monologue, which I'd love to quote in full here, but can't because film studios have more money for copyright attorneys than book authors do.)

Peter was onto something. Psychological studies *do* show that we have a terrible time discerning reality from what we see on TV. Our brains were "designed" to interpret what we see and hear as actually being in the world because for most of human history this was true. Where else could an image be generated except in the real world?

Media celebrities are a recent phenomena because *media* is a recent phenomenon. Before recorded music and film, only those close enough to a theater could experience a theatrical performance. Books and newspapers record stories of theatrical pioneers, great singers, musicians, and dancers, but there is no way to experience their performances today. The technologies of the late nineteenth and twentieth centuries allowed people, for the first time, to hear music and drama miles and years from where they were initially performed. For the first time a farmer in Kansas could experience the work of the same artists as a factory worker in Chicago. It also created much more enduring celebrity icons. Memories of Vaudeville performers faded, and their fame disappeared, but thanks to film, Rudolf Valentino lives on—and we feel we know him. Our brains don't know the difference.

This explains why stalkers occasionally show up in TV stars' kitchens claiming to be their wives. Of course, identification with fictional characters is nothing new. As Steve Allen pointed out in his book, *Dumpth*, back in the 1940s, studies showed that when a character on a soap-opera had a life event, such as a wedding or a pregnancy, thousands of listeners would send the types of gifts that would be appropriate to send to real friends in such cases. "If a soap-opera character had a baby, she would receive enormous quantities of booties, little caps or jackets, supplies of diapers, cards of congratulations, and so on," Allen wrote. "I was very young when I learned this, but I have never forgotten how the news depressed me. It still does."

What is different is the immediacy of television—its ability to stim-ulate our visual neural pathways. The moving images on a television screen trigger a primitive "orienting response." We're programmed to turn and watch what is moving so that we're not devoured by a saber-toothed tiger. With the fast edits and action scenes that came in with the Sesame Street and MTV generation, our orienting reflexes are now activated about once per second when we sit in front of the telly. The result is a quasi-hypnotic state.

Research shows that people who watch trauma on television have the same physical symptoms, such as elevated blood pressure and heart rate, as if the person has actually experienced the trauma. In case you needed a scientist to tell you this: Research shows that the people who watched the most television coverage of the events of September 11, 2001, reported the most stress. And people who watch TV news, which relishes reporting violent crime, believe their cities are increasingly violent, even when the level of violence decreases.

Whether this perception is entirely wrong is a philosophical ques-tion. Most of our free time today is taken up by TV viewing. We spend much more time in front of the box than out on the street. So the odds are quite small that we'll ever witness a violent crime outside the home. Yet the chance that we will witness acts of violence in our living rooms is astonishingly high as we choose our entertainment from among the various *CSI* and *Law & Order* franchise offerings. Fictional Las Vegas and New York are dangerous places indeed, and most of us will spend more time there than in the real cities they represent.

The facts: Americans say that TV is the least necessary part of their lives, yet they devote more time to it than to any other leisure activity. In one survey in the 1980s, U.S. residents overwhelmingly dubbed TV programming "dull and repetitive." They estimate that they have less than twenty hours of free time a week, yet they also report watching twenty-one hours of television a week.

Television bombards us with vivid commercial images urging us to desire material goods. "For the first time in history," wrote professor and media critic George Gerbner, "most children are born into homes where most of the stories do not come from their parents, schools churches, communities, and in many places even from their native countries, but from a handful of conglomerates who have something to sell."

The beloved children's entertainer Bob Keeshan, better known as Captain Kangaroo, put it more succinctly: "Television is not a tool for nurturing. It is a tool for selling." (Then Mr. Moose told a knock-knock joke and an avalanche of ping pong balls fell on his head.)

While the advertising aspect of TV gets most of the attention and criticism, it is only part of the problem. Even if you use that nifty new DVR to zap through the commercials, television is still transporting you into a world of unreality and heightened expectations.

You see, we do not judge how we should be living by logical analysis of what we need. We determine what we should have by looking at our neighbors. Today our neighbors do not live next door, they live on Wisteria Lane. We're not trying to keep up with the Joneses any more. We're trying to keep up with the Kardashians.

Today, the most common dreams of young people are acting, sports, music, and screenwriting. Almost 1 out of 20 college students, according to a 2004 survey, plans on becoming an actor, artist, or musician. This is more than want to be lawyers, nurses, accountants, business owners, journalists, or high school teachers. Given a choice between fame and contentment 29 percent of 1990's young people chose fame. (Back in the late 1960s, more than 80 percent of entering college freshmen in one survey listed as their most important academic goal: "developing a meaningful philosophy of life." Isn't that quaint?)

"'Following your dreams' sounds like a good principle," wrote Jean Twenge in *Generation Me*, "until you realize that every waiter in L.A. is following his or her dreams of becoming an actor, and most of them won't succeed. Most people are not going to realize their dreams because most people do not dream of becoming accountants, social workers, or trash collectors.... And few dream of the white-collar jobs in business that many of us have or will have."

It has been estimated that in the medieval world the average person saw one hundred other people in the course of a *lifetime*. In a world where it is quite possible to know everyone you encounter, there is no such thing as "fame" in the sense we understand it today. There were, of course, prominent members of the community—religious leaders, soldiers, kings. To have real fame, however, requires something more impersonal. The famous are people we all know of, but few of us know.

Gossip plays an important role in human society, and it has since the days of our tribal ancestors. We used stories about the other members of our clans to measure our status in society and to forge alliances. People supply information to people to whom they are attracted or interested. A bit of gossip cements a relationship and a place in the hierarchy. While our brains are still programmed for a stone-age tribal world, our society has changed. In nineteenth-century China, women had a novel solution to the problem—professional gossipers. Wealthy Chinese women of the time, by reasons of social mores and bound feet, did not travel much. Elderly women, usually widows, supported themselves by going from home to home getting and spreading tales about the people of society.

Our feet may not be bound, but modern Westerners are just as cut off from the majority of people in society. Our populations are simply too large for everyone in a major city or even a medium-sized town to know everyone's business. To fill our need for gossip we turn to entertainment, sports, and television to provide common reference points—individuals we all "know" whether we are from the same "clan" or not. A person from Manhattan can discuss Michael Jackson's death with someone from Iowa or even England. Tom Cruise's leap on Oprah's couch becomes our common currency.

We tend to associate celebrity identification with women. The typical example is a lonely, middle-aged, working class woman who can't distinguish her soap opera characters from real peers.

But our TV confusion is hardly limited to female fans of fashion icons and daytime drama. Armchair sports fans often take credit for a victory as if they actually played the game: "We won!" As if watching the game from the comfort of a barc-a-lounger somehow spurred the team to a touchdown. Psychological studies have shown that die-hard sports fans sometimes identify so closely with their team that a loss on the field can lead to depression or a serious blow to self-esteem. Some anthropologists have compared the rush of emotions and hormones during a sporting match with that of a male animal battling over a female.

Thanks to TV, we are all hanging out with celebrities on a daily basis, at least somewhere in the uncritical emotional part of our minds. It wouldn't be such a problem for our self-esteem if our imaginary neighbor was Mr. Rogers. More frequently, however, we're shacking up with the Millionaire Matchmaker. We could be spending time sitting on milk crates in our friend's unfinished basement apartment, but we're at home watching MTV's *Cribs* and thinking our two-bedroom place is an embarrassing pig sty.

How better to make this point than to let a fictional character take the honors: Tyler Durden (played by Brad Pitt) in the movie *Fight Club* said, "Our generation has had no Great Depression, no Great War. Our depression is our lives. . . . We were raised on television to believe that we'd all be millionaires, movie gods, rock stars, but we won't. And we're starting to figure that out. And we're very, very pissed off."

Part of our TV attraction to millionaires is simple voyeurism. We like to gawk at mansions and possessions and imagine owning a designer wardrobe like Carrie in *Sex and the City*. Robin Leach once said that he called his program *Lifestyles of the Rich and Famous* because if it was called *Lifestyles of the Poor and Unknown* no one would watch.

But there is something else at play—the need to attract an affluent audience who will buy lots of stuff and make commercial time worth the investment.

The great art of Europe was commissioned by kings and nobles, who could spend their money on whatever pleased them. They did not have shareholders to answer to—and they were, as the wealthy of all times have been, concerned with their own amusement and self-aggrandizement. They supported arts and artists to uplift them, entertain them, and sing their praises. When we got rid of the kings, we got rid of our traditional method of funding the arts.

With no kings around, it fell on business to take up the slack. That meant that our arts had to attract the widest possible audience to be profitable. Arts became entertainment, something else to consume. This made it hard for classical arts like ballet to get a toe hold in our culture. And it explains why the Bravo TV network morphed from a commercial-free fine arts channel that aired plays and symphonies in the 1980s to reality-TV central in the 1990s. (*Inside the Actors Studio* and the name Bravo are the only two fossils of its fine arts past.)

For every artist with a brilliant idea for an innovative new show for the fall season, there is a business executive who has to answer the question, "Will it sell soap (or cars or Viagra)?" If it won't, the network will go out of business and your set will go dark. Where would you be then? You might have to read a book or go talk to a friend. Nobody wants that to happen.

And nobody is in the business to put out mind-numbingly bland pap and pabulum to hypnotize the masses. The actors, directors, writers, and producers are in the business to tell stories. Some of them probably have visions of changing our perceptions of the world with groundbreaking and innovative new ideas and artistic concepts.

But to get permission to show their work—and deliver it at no cost to you!—they have made a deal with advertisers who want access to your brain for marketing messages. In return for your eyeballs on the screen when the word *Ford* flashes, the corporation will fund the creation and distribution of your entertainment.

Thus, quality television, in industry terms, is programming that will draw affluent viewers.

"I once visited a successful Hollywood producer," wrote novelist John Gardner in *Esquire*, "and he gave me a list of what 'the American people don't like.' They've done marketing research and they know. The American people don't like movies with snowy landscapes. The American people don't like movies about farmers. The American people don't like movies in which the central characters are foreigners. The list went on, but I stopped listening, because the movie I'd come to talk about concerned a Vietnamese immigrant family's first winter in Iowa."

What do affluent Americans like, according to the studies? Wealthy people like themselves—or better yet, characters they aspire to be, in similar lines of white-collar work, but just a bit richer, better dressed, sexier, and more glamorous.

It is a world of art left to the professionals, of images of bodies of sculpted perfection, of the packaged and polished. In that atmosphere, anything that has not passed through editors and filters seems flawed and dirty. Even our "reality television" is sponsored and buffed and tied up with a bow.

In their article "Lifestyles of the Rich and Famous: Does Television Make Us More Materialistic," researchers L. J. Shrum of the University of Texas at San Antonio, James E. Burroughs of the University of Virginia, and Aric Rindfleisch of the University of Wisconsin-Madison observe: "Television portrays wealth and affluence frequently and positively. . . . The world of television is a much wealthier, more affluent one than the real world. Few popular television programs (other than the occasional movie or documentary) focus on poor people. One may find programs that feature 'working class' characters, but even a close examination of these characters' lives usually shows them to be getting by quite well."

In case you didn't guess what the researchers concluded, here it is: There is a correlation between TV viewing and increased materialism. The more you watch, the more you want.

The result? A survey conducted in the early 1990s found that 85 percent of American households aspired to a lifestyle associated with those in the top fifth of the income ladder.

What I'm saying is if you were to shell out for that big-screen TV, you would just end up desiring a bigger screen TV in a few weeks.

Sister Carol Anne O'Marie is a nun in Oakland, California, who writes mystery novels about an elderly nun playing detective. According to Leigh Winers of the *San Jose Mercury*, Sister O'Marie was once approached by a Hollywood company to turn her novels into a television series. The executives loved the story, but wanted to tweak a few details. For example, instead of a grandmotherly *Murder She Wrote* type, perhaps the main character could be young and sexy. It would be more dramatic if she had a colorful past, perhaps a drinking or drug problem and an illicit love affair before she joined the convent. O'Marie was flattered by the offer, but couldn't see making those kind of changes to her story. "You're turning down a chance, Sister, to make a lot of money," the executive told her.

"What would I do with it?" replied O'Marie, who had taken a vow of poverty. "I'm not going to live in a nicer convent."

Daydreams Are Like Free Movies

"People think of fantasy as different from reality, but fantasy is almost like the reality that will come. Everyone creates the fantasies, so everyone creates the reality."

—YOKO ONO, JAPANESE-AMERICAN ARTIST

Movies are expensive. Theater is for the rich. Even video rentals cost $4. Save your money. There is an alternative that not only costs nothing, it requires no expensive multimedia equipment and needs no electricity to run. I'm talking about daydreaming. You can enjoy daydreaming in a comfortable home or a homeless shelter. In fact, it is probably more satisfying to imagine yourself a king when you're living in the back of a car than when you're living in a mansion.

Are you sick to death of seeing Brad Pitt? Think Quentin Tarintino should take his blood and gore and go home? Believe you could make a better film than Steven Spielberg? No problem. Give it your best shot, and if your movie sucks, no one will know. Not only is it absolutely free to screen epics on your gray matter, you have total creative control. Your fantasies are never interrupted by commercials, no one is ever miscast, and you get to play the leading man in the sex scene with Catherine Zeta-Jones. (Or the leading lady to Hugh Jackman—or the leading man to Hugh Jackman, for that matter. Whatever floats your boat.) It is better than Hollywood, because there is no one you can't work with. Even death does not make someone unavailable for your project. You can dance with Fred Astaire in his prime—and keep up! And it might just give you some fresh ideas about who you want to be in the "real world."

Several years ago I took a bus trip to see a Woody Guthrie exhibit at a major museum in New York City with a group of volunteers and friends from The Guthrie Center, a Massachusetts non-profit organization founded by Arlo Guthrie (son of Woody).

Woody Guthrie lived with migrant workers and penned political songs about the things he saw and the ordinary working folk he met during the Depression era. He was an inspiration to a generation of 1960s folk singers, notably Bob Dylan. (If you're broke, I recommend developing a taste for the working man's anthems of 1930s folk musicians and blues singers. They'll make you feel noble.)

In the center of the Woody Guthrie exhibit was a biographical film, the main thrust of which was that Guthrie had been an inspiration to a lot of people. What I remember most about this film was musician Billy Bragg talking about a song Guthrie had written in which he said when he died he just wanted to be remembered as "another man gone." He wanted the words to matter, but he was not personally important. In the middle of a Woody Guthrie museum exhibit, it was charmingly ironic. (Almost as good as Abraham Lincoln's words from the Gettysburg Address, "the world will little note nor long remember what we say here," which are carved in stone at the Lincoln Memorial.)

Another musician in the film talked about people like Bob Dylan being a "link in the folk music chain," and Woody Guthrie was "the hook that holds the chain in the ground." I have to differ. Woody Guthrie's legacy is not in question. But the tradition he represents, that of telling stories and putting them into song, goes back to the beginnings of humanity. Long before there was television or the Internet, before there were records or even recorded history, people were sharing music. Woody Guthrie came along when radio was new and recordings were rudimentary. He is not the hook in the ground of folk music, but the hook in the ground of the age when the folk tradition was recorded for posterity instead of just spoken and sung. Whether it was his aspiration or not, Woody Guthrie was one of the first *non-anonymous* folk singers.

These days we've become accustomed to the idea that entertainment is something you consume, not something you make. We buy records, we rent DVDs, and we generally leave imagination to the professionals. Much of modern life, in fact, seems to be a rebellion against daydreaming. We listen to radio on the way to and from work; we switch on the TV the minute we get home. There are now even screens to entertain us in restaurants and at the gas pump, as if we would become so bored in the five minutes it takes to pump gas that we would just give up and go home. They should know that's never going to happen. That's what iPods are for.

How are we ever to find a moment for quality daydreaming with the CNN airport network and the CNN grocery store check-out line network and CNN monitors at the post office? Recent surveys show that children everywhere now spend up to 80 percent of their free time outside of school watching television. Not surprisingly kids who are heavy TV viewers are less imaginative than children who watch only one hour a day. We no longer value our own fantasies; we pay other people to show us theirs.

This is a shame, because dreaming stuff up is what human beings do best. Our brains differ from our fellow creatures in the animal kingdom in one notable way: *we imagine the future*. Paleontologists tell us that about three million years ago the human brain went through a dramatic transformation and nearly doubled its mass in a little more than two million years. The one-and-a-half-pound brain of Homo habilis grew to three pounds in the Homo sapiens. A disproportionate share of this growth was devoted to the frontal lobe. This part of the brain, which is also the slowest to mature, is responsible for our ability to plan.

Patients who have suffered injuries to the frontal lobe function perfectly normally in most respects, except one. They have no concept of "tomorrow." They understand the word *tomorrow* and know that there is a passage of time, but what they will be *doing* tomorrow is completely incomprehensible to them. In 1981, a psychologist interviewed a patient with this sort of brain injury and asked him what he thought about when he was asked to think about "tomorrow." The patient said it was like "being in a room with nothing there and having a guy tell you to go find a chair."

"We think about the future in a way that no other animal can, does, or ever has," wrote Harvard psychologist Daniel Gilbert in *Stumbling on Happiness*, "and this simple, ubiquitous, ordinary act is a defining feature of our humanity."

Yet in a culture totally devoted to activity, the daydream has gotten a bad rap. Psychology textbooks used to warn that excessive daydreaming can propel a person into insanity, and during World War I, a U.S. army questionnaire included the statement "I daydream frequently" to weed out neurotic recruits.

We think of a daydreamer as an unproductive slacker, someone who would rather escape to a fantasy world than deal with his responsibilities in this one. Scientists are coming to a different point of view. In fact, they now see the daydreaming mind as "the default network." It is what the brain "defaults" to in the absence of mental stimulation from the outside world. Neurologist Marcus Raichle of Washington University in St. Louis calls the default network the "backbone of consciousness."

This is why those "a-ha!" moments seem to come when we have nothing better to do, when we're stuck in traffic, dozing off to sleep, or taking a shower. It's why Archimedes shouted "Eureka!" and went running through the streets naked after a scientific epiphany in the bathtub, and why Kary Mullins, who discovered a method of replicating DNA, first conceived of the idea on a long drive between San Francisco and his cabin in the Mendocino woods. If Albert Einstein hadn't been bored with his job at the Swiss patent office, he might never have gazed out the window and imagined himself running alongside a light wave, a musing that led to the theory of relativity.

Now that scientists can observe brain activity using MRIs, they have discovered that during daydreaming, the part of the brain associated with complex problem-solving is actually working harder than it is during focused concentration. When people say, "stop daydreaming and focus on the task at hand," they are being coun-terproductive.

"People assume that when the mind wanders away it gets turned off, but we show the opposite, that when it wanders, it turns on," neu-roscientist Kalina Christoff told MX Sydney. "People who let themselves daydream might not think in the same focused ways when performing a goal-oriented task, but they bring in more mental and brain resources."

Daydreams help us develop our sense of self and rehearse our social skills, and they are a key component of creativity. Successful innovators are often those who pay the most attention to the wisdom that comes in the form of mental meanderings.

". . . A book provides for a distillation of our sporadic mind," wrote author Alain DeBotton, "a record of its most vital manifestations, a con-centration of inspired moments that might originally have arisen across a multitude of years and been separated by extended stretches of bovine gazing."

Far from being an unproductive waste of time, those "stretches of bovine gazing" are, in fact, what make creative innovation possible. As we drift into a stream of consciousness, our minds drift from topic to topic, mixing the past, present, and future, drawing on elements from our internal and external worlds. This mix leads to the kind of new con-nections that lead to innovation.

THINGS TO BE THANKFUL FOR

At least they're not playing bagpipes. A Scottish debt collector sends a bagpipe player in full regalia to the homes of its deadbeats to shame them into coughing up. Other humiliating collection agencies include the Spanish El Cobrador del Frac, "The Debt Collector in Top Hat and Tails," who arrive in costume in a well marked van, and The Monastary of Collection, which sends out workers dressed as Franciscan friars who chant until the debts are paid.

26

Shiny Happy People: The Joneses Are Doing Worse Than You Think (They Just Have Good PR)

"Men are greedy to publish the successes of their efforts, but meanly shy as to publishing the failures of men. Men are ruined by this one-sided practice of concealment of blunders and failures."

—ABRAHAM LINCOLN

Before she was the *Million Dollar Baby*, actress Hilary Swank embodied Tina Brandon in the small film *Boys Don't Cry*. It was a career breakthrough for the actress, netting her an Oscar.

After the parties ended and the gown went back to the designer, Swank went to the pharmacy to fill a prescription. It cost $280. She presented her insurance card, but was denied. The pharmacy knew she was an Academy Award–winning actress, and they sheepishly tried to run the card a few more times to no avail. Swank left the pharmacy without her prescription and called the insurance company. They explained that you had to earn a certain amount to qualify for the Screen Actor's Guild insurance plan. At that time, the minimum to qualify was $5,000. For her powerful performance in "Boys Don't Cry," Swank was paid just $75 a day, for a grand total of $3,000.

"So I had an Academy Award, and I didn't have health insurance," she told Mike Wallace. "The life of an actor."

We find this story ironic because in our culture it simply doesn't compute. We associate the terms *rich* and *famous*. We have nowhere to mentally file *poor and famous*. Yet it happens much more frequently than you might think.

The problem is that most of the time, when it does, people work rather hard to conceal the embarrassing fact.

From its origins with Horatio Alger to its supremacy in Hollywood blockbusters, we have come to expect stories that unfold in a particular way. Here are two things I know from watching movies.

1. If a man and a woman meet and they can't stand each other, they will fall in love.
2. If a person is a poor, misunderstood underdog, he will triumph in the end.

You probably know enough men and women who can't stand each other when they meet and keep right on hating each other all their lives to disprove the first hypothesis. The second one is a little trickier, because we conspire with it in our everyday lives. We serve as our own little PR agencies broadcasting our achievements and spinning the failures.

Out of all of the academic terminology I jotted down for 101 classes in college, my favorite was "phatic communication."* It refers to those pieces of conversation that convey absolutely no information; they simply serve a social function. For example: If we didn't say "hello" we'd have to blurt out "I recognize that you are another human being in the room."

When you need to move beyond that to "I recognize that you are a person I have met before," the standard greeting is, "how are you?" If *My Fair Lady* is to be believed, the posh British (and presumably the pretentious Americans) say "how do you do?" To which the answer is also "how do you do?"

After a few conversations like this:

"How do you do?"
"How do you do?"
"How do you do?"
"How do you do?"

Us plebes abandoned the practice of answering a question with a question.

Of course, there is still actually only one correct answer to "how are you?," and that is to say that you are doing well.

"How are you?"
"Fine."

---

*my second favorite was "nominal fallacy," which is the mistaken belief that by giving something a name you have explained something about it.

There is a famous quotation that the definition of a bore is someone who, when you ask how they are, actually tells you.

I discovered an interesting exception when my father died. In the weeks surrounding the funeral, the question subtly changed. When someone dies, someone close to you, they don't ask "how are you?" but "how are you *doing?*"

The "doing" is an acknowledgment that "how are you?" is a non-question. When we ask "how are you?" we don't want to know. "How are you?" is short for "I see that you are here and I would like to engage you in conversation."

"How are you *doing?*" expresses that the querant has heard your bad news, and actually cares. Of course, even when we are grieving, we don't really answer such a question with information. It's just not done. When the question is "how are you *doing?*" instead of a standard "fine" you pause and say "Okay"

Pause and "Okay" means things are terrible. "I'm barely holding on. I don't know if I can make it through this." Pause. "Okay."

After "hello" and "how are you?" chit chat gets a little more complicated. If you don't want to talk about the weather—

"Cold enough for you?"

"Temperatures appear to be in the normal climatic range. The total precipitation is below normal and the snowfall is expected to be near normal for the rest of the week."

Then you get into some dangerous territory:

"So what is new with you? What have you been up to lately?"

"What is new with you?" seems like an innocent question in the same category as "how are you?," but don't be fooled. Most people spend their entire lives in the quest to have a good answer the next time they are confronted with that question at a social gathering.

You want your answer to be something along the lines of: "I just got back from a professional conference in Geneva where I was discussing a new research breakthrough that could change the way vaccines are distributed in third-world nations."

That's what you want to be able to say. Chances are, though, your answer is going to be more along the lines of "Well, I was up for a promotion, but they hired someone from outside. I thought about quitting, but, you know. Still, I think I might be getting a couple extra vacation days next year."

With a simple "what have you been up to?" you can tell immediately who is happy with his life and who isn't. One of two things will happen—the other speaker's eyes may get wide, she'll stand a little taller, lean in, and speak quickly, "We just found out we're pregnant!" Or her shoulders will slump, her eyes will be cast to her shoes, and she'll say, "Well, I'm kind of between things at the moment."

It is a glaringly personal question. Yet the momentum of social convention makes us ask it—even when we really don't care. When I was young, my family moved a lot. I went to four different high schools so I didn't really know most of the people in my graduating class. Years later, a friend, one of the few I'd kept in touch with, invited me to go to our high school reunion. I went, mostly to keep her company. I didn't recognize any of these people, and yet I found myself asking over and over, "So what have you been up to?" They would answer with this or that, they worked here, they married so-and-so, they were attending graduate school. I always wanted to follow up with, "Uh-huh, and by the way, what were you doing back then?"

The irony is that many of them were probably agonizing over the answer to the question, comparing the words they were saying to the dream of what their answers would be when they were in back in high school. (Given how few rock stars there were at the reunion, I'm assuming many people had made some changes in their goals).

The thing is that even when you have a perfectly good answer to the question of "what are you doing now?" It never seems to get to the heart of things. You never quite feel that you are able to respond with what really matters. We talk about our jobs, our achievements, our social status; but rarely about the things that truly sustain us—our relationships, our current obsessions, our souls. That would, of course, be a lot to ask from a little phatic communication. Most of the time it is enough to recognize there is another human being in the room.

Literature doesn't do much to dispel the notion that we're all doing fine either. When I read Henry David Thoreau's *Walden*, I could not help but feel a longing for his quiet life of contemplation. The prose and the praise for simplicity and an authentic life struck a deep chord. But I also found Thoreau to be a little bit smug about his lifestyle. Not everyone, I reasoned, had the luxury of chucking it all and living "deliberately" in the woods to "suck all the marrow out of life." It turns out, neither did Thoreau. *Walden* did not spring full blown from the top of Thoreau's head one afternoon. It was edited and tweaked over years. It also glosses over the author's work life. Like many artists, Thoreau supported himself with a variety of odd jobs. He reported the the secretary of his Harvard class in 1847 that he was "a School master—a Private Tutor, a Surveyor—a Gardener, a Farmer—a Painter, I mean a House Painter, a Carpenter, a Mason, a Day-Laborer, a Pencil-Maker, a Glass-paper Maker, a Writer and sometimes a Poetaster." And on and off as an adult he lived with his father.

Ever wonder how travel writers can afford to take a year or two off and travel from coast to coast? Most of them can't. They can, however, take a trip for a week or a month and a weekend here and there. Then they piece together the tale in a seamless uninterrupted narrative. You read and dream of their romantic life and wonder when you'll have the time and means to imitate them. Everyone but you, it seems, is *doing fine.*

"Artists use frauds to make human beings seem more wonderful than they really are," wrote Kurt Vonnegut. "Dancers show us human beings who move much more gracefully than human beings really move. Films and books and plays show us people talking much more entertainingly than people really talk, making paltry human enterprises seem important. Singers and musicians show us human beings making sounds far more lovely than human beings really make. Architects give us temples in which something marvelous is obviously going on. Actually, practically nothing is going on."

We are all shaped, whether we admit it or not, by the American story of rags to riches and triumph over adversity. I once asked a Russian ballet dancer friend what the "Russian story" was. His answer blew my mind. Of course he is not a scholar, and not an expert, but this is what came to his mind as the typical Russian tale: Boy meets girl. Boy dies. Boy comes back as a ghost. They live (or is it die?) happily ever after and there is a lesson, a moral.

The hero of the Russian story *dies* before it has even gotten interesting! The American story is about winning. The Russian story is about what you learn from losing. American heroes continue in the face of all obstacles. They do not waver, and eventually win through sheer force of character and will. Russian heroes are cut down before they even have a chance to begin. Then the hero is reborn to the circumstances, he is victorious in failure and he brings his lesson back to the world.

The American story does not teach us what to do with failure. It simply does not give us the option. Villains fail. Heroes succeed. The problem is that in real life bad things do happen to good people. So perhaps we don't need any more stories of heroes winning against insurmountable odds. Perhaps we need stories that tell us we'll come out on the other side of our failures.

Appearing always to be happy is an American virtue. We have little patience for a glum sourpuss or the situation that put him there. Everywhere you turn there are self-help books, talk shows, and televangelists promising to make you happy.

The British in particular have turned the expression "Have a nice day," pronounced with an American accent, into a parody of U.S. consumer culture. There's something about all that friendliness that rubs the English the wrong way. One letter writer to the *London Times* said: "During my chairmanship of the Campaign for Courtesy, interviewers would often ask: 'But we don't want to go down the American 'have a nice day' route, do we?"

If you take a cue from other cultures and accept that unhappiness is often normal, then you may be much better emotionally equipped to cope with those penniless days.

Gold into Lead

No matter how bad your luck, it must be better than that of John Sutter. Things seemed to be going well for Sutter in 1826 when he married his sweetheart, Anna Dubelt, and started his own cloth and yarn business. But the business went belly-up and Sutter was forced to leave his wife and four children behind to seek his fortune in America. He would send for his family as soon as he was able. First, he sailed to Missouri, but his boat was wrecked, and once again, Sutter lost everything. In 1839, he found himself in a region that was then part of Mexico. He built a settlement there with a fort called Sutter's Fort and a mill called Sutter's Mill. In January 1848, Sutter's partner, James Marshall, discovered gold at the mill. One would think that discovery of gold on your land would be a great stroke of luck, and at first it seemed to be that way. Sutter sent for his family in 1849, just as the '49ers started to converge on his property. Sutter's Mill was overrun by prospectors and people hoping to cash in on the prospectors. Sutter spent most of his remaining years in court trying to prove his claim to the land, but the Supreme Court finally ruled that they were invalid. Sutter, whose name had become synonymous with gold, died broke and despondent.

27

Cloak of Invisibility: Poor and Anonymous. It's a Good Thing

....

"Better to be forgotten than sued."

—DAVE WEINBAUM, COMEDIAN

Imagine for a moment that you are bitten by a radioactive spider and discover that you now have a superhuman power to render yourself invisible at will. What would you do? Would you sneak into the White House to see what goes on behind closed doors? Would you go into your boss's office and move things around? Would you, like Clay Aiken in the song "Invisible", go and watch the object of your affection doing whatever she does in her room at night? (Anyone else find this song a little stalker-creepy?)

Factoid: Marvel Comics hero The Invisible Woman joined The Fantastic Four in 1961. She may have been there before, but nobody could see her.

The cloak of invisibility is a common pop culture fantasy. We love to imagine what it would be like to go all those places we are not permitted to go; to see unseen.

In an article in *Americana: The Journal of American Popular Culture,* John Lennon (no relation) of Lehigh University wrote about the fabled hobo ridin' the rails.

"By stealing a ride, hobos are outside of history," he wrote. "There is no seat assigned, no money exchanged for a ticket, no knowledge that they are even there on the train, and therefore, they do not officially exist. And while the railroad engineers may suspect that the hobos are there, they do not count. When people exist in the spaces of society . . . those who are connected to places will not recognize them. . . . [Michel De Certeau, author of *The Practice of Everyday Life*] correctly wrote that 'history exists where there is a price to be paid.'"

People's pupils dilate when they're in the presence of celebrities and millionaires. Wouldn't you snap to immediate attention if Barack Obama or Paul McCartney suddenly walked through the door? Yet we barely acknowledge the custodian working in the hall, the garbage collector out on the street, or the kid who rings up our Big Mac. (Here's a free tip for law enforcement from my days as a pizza delivery driver: If you want to catch people using pot, go under cover as the pizza guy. The folks with the munchies never bother to put their stuff away because the pizza guy isn't like a real person at the door. People open the door in their pajamas and undershorts. They also assume the pizza guy is going to be a *guy*.)

As a broke person, you are often invisible, and it can be a good thing. There is something to be said for having an opportunity to observe without being observed. Looking from an outsider's perspective is much more creative than hanging out with the big boys and swallowing their Kool-Aid ™.

Gordon MacKenzie wrote a wonderful little book called *Orbiting the Giant Hairball.* The titular hairball is the corporate group-think that grows in an organization over time. Corporations don't begin as giant hairballs. They begin life as simple, effective concepts, one or two strands of the ideas that will produce success. As success builds on success, more and more strands of "things that have worked in the past" get woven together. Next thing you know, you've got a giant hairball.

"It is a common history of enterprises to begin in a state of naïve groping, stumble onto success, milk the success with a vengeance, and, in the process, generate systems that arrogantly turn away from the source of their original success: groping," MacKenzie wrote.

Picture Michael Douglas delivering this line: "The point is, ladies and gentleman, that groping—for lack of a better word—is good. Groping is right. Groping works. Groping clarifies, cuts through, and captures the essence of the evolutionary spirit. Groping, in all of its forms—groping for life, for money, for love, knowledge—has marked the upward surge of mankind. And groping—you mark my words—will not only save Teldar Paper, but that other malfunctioning corporation called the USA."

The hairball explains the embarrassing fact that the greatest inventions of history normally come from individuals not formally educated in the field where they achieve their breakthroughs. For example, Darwin's theory of evolution was not the work of an archaeologist. Louis Pasteur was not a medical doctor.

A musician invented Kodachrome film. A sculptor created the ballpoint pen. A veterinarian came up with the pneumatic tire. An undertaker invented automatic telephones. Two bicycle mechanics fashioned the first airplane. And a sixteen-year-old high school student invented the television. And minorities, outside of the establishment, have made many inventive breakthroughs. African-Americans, for example, invented the traffic signal, fire extinguisher, automatic gear shifting, refrigeration, and discovered blood plasma.

The introduction to the Anita Barrows and Joanna Macy translation of Rainer Rilke's *Book of Hours* (subtitled *Love Poems to God*) explained that, in his lifetime, the poems were "intimate, sacred to him, unmentioned in his letters and even in his journal." Had his poetry been visible in his lifetime, it may have lacked the very sacredness, the very personal nature that makes it truthful and meaningful to so many today.

The value of outsider status is in "intelligent ignorance"—contributions by people who haven't yet been brainwashed into knowing what is "impossible" or how things have "always been done." As someone once said, "We don't know who first discovered water, but we can be sure it wasn't a fish."

"I see more of what is going on around me because I am not concerned with finding a parking place."

—QUOTED IN TAXI DRIVER WISDOM, **BY RISA MICKENBERG**

To preserve groping, Gordon MacKenzie proposes "orbiting" the hairball, staying within its general sphere of influence, without being sucked in by its established patterns.

"Orbiting is responsible creativity," he wrote, "vigorously exploring and operating beyond the Hairball of the corporate mindset, beyond 'accepted models, patterns, or standards'—all the while remaining connected to the spirit of the corporate mission."

Of course, some people *like* the hairball. If you're still not sure what you want to be when you grow up, a corporate bureaucracy can be a great way to find security in the form of titles and status without actual responsibility. The buck stops somewhere else. So says James H. Boren, who coined the collective term "a mumble of bureaucrats" (like a herd of cattle, a flock of sheep, or an exaltation of larks).

"Action and logic are the principal causes of disruptive rippling in the seas of institutional tranquility," he wrote in his book, *Fuzzify*. "The image of productivity, however, preserves tranquility and permits career enhancement without causing a ripple or even a bubble. In some situations, image can be more real than reality itself."

We spend so much time and effort building up a public persona, energy that could be put to better use in pursuit of something authentic. In America, we try to project an optimistic, happy person who is affluent, upwardly mobile, and in control of her destiny. We put so much energy into staging our show that we rarely stop to wonder who our audience is supposed to be. Exactly who do we think is buying a ticket?

When John Lennon (the musical one) uttered the phrase, "We're more famous than Jesus Christ now," it caused a scandal. Christians burned Beatles records. The Fab Four were booed and banned. But

Lennon may well have been right —after all, the majority of the world's people (67 percent) are not Christian.*

Nevertheless, the Beatle was dismayed at the reaction to his off-hand comment. In a press conference he explained, "I'm not saying that we're better or greater, or comparing us with Jesus Christ as a person or God as a thing or whatever it is. . . . I wasn't saying whatever they're saying I was saying."

The outcry over the Beatles and Jesus quote tells more about how Americans (the outcry was mostly from Americans) value *fame* than how they value *religion*. Fame is universally viewed as a positive. Fame is good. The most famous man must be the greatest man, and the greatest the most famous.

> **Factoid:** In 1998, *Time Magazine* published a 75th anniversary issue. It included a list of the most collectible back issues of the magazine and the prices they fetched, some as high as $1,000. The price of collectible magazines is largely based on who is on the cover. *Time* noted: "with athletes, entertainers and Nazis especially prized."

When Elizabeth Edwards, wife of former presidential candidate John Edwards appeared on the *Oprah Winfrey Show* to discuss her book on coping with her husband's infidelity, she made only one

---

*FYI— The Vatican forgave Lennon for his 1966 comment . . . in November 2008.

request—that Oprah not mention the other woman's name. She didn't want to reward the woman with what we all understand to be the prize of the spotlight. But was the public eye really a boon for, say, Monica Lewinsky? Is fame for its own sake really worth having?

We have a deeply held cultural assumption that it is best to be best known. But being singled out is also to be alone. It is in our smallness that we are bound to all other people, not in our grandness. The drive to be exceptional is just one more thing that keeps us isolated in modern society.

When I did public relations for a major classical ballet touring company, I had to convince entertainment reporters to give as much coverage to Swan Lake as to another show that was touring at the time: *The Puppetry of the Penis*. That was a performance piece in which two naked Australian men folded their penises and scrotums into different shapes. It was tough for *Swan Lake* to compete with that. (Even if the men would be wearing tights.)

Inevitably the reporter wanted to know what was new and different about our production of *Swan Lake*. I went on about new interpretations and set pieces, but the real answer, the non-PR answer, is that there was nothing new about it. If you want new, try *Puppetry of the Penis*. You go to *Swan Lake* to see something old.

In a culture that tends to emphasize the new and novel, it has sometimes been a hard sell to explain the appeal of ballet's "moldy oldies." Paradoxically, it is only by comparison with the great dancers of the past who have executed these same solos and *pas de deux* that a dancer's true nature shines most fully. The familiarity of the material emphasizes her differences, the uniqueness of her interpretation and animating spirit.

In this sense it is ritual, just as we pass through an experience such as a wedding. The bridal gown would be nothing but a white dress if it didn't carry with it the weight of all those brides of the past, of the grandmothers long gone, who were once young and in love and beginning a life with a partner. You don't wear the dress because it makes you *unique*, but because it makes you the *same*—it ties you to all the others. The spotlight never shines for you alone. But it is your moment to carry the bright torch of life. The invisible are bound together.

> **Asked by a reporter to put into 25 words or less what he is trying to say when he gets up on stage, Joe Strummer of the rock band The Clash replied, "Look At Me!"**

28

Reasons to Be Glad You Can't Afford to Live in a Good Neighborhood

"The law, in its majestic equality, forbids the rich as well as the poor to sleep under bridges."

—ANATOLE FRANCE, FRENCH AUTHOR

If you like to read good escapist fantasy, I recommend picking up a book called *The One Minute Millionaire*. Ostensibly a self-help business book, it is actually a lottery ticket in book form. Written by the creator of the *Chicken Soup for the Soul* book series, it is an extended pep talk that promises you, too, can go from rags to riches. During the time you're reading it, you'll be ready to tell your boss where to go and prepare for your new life as a millionaire. It wears off fairly quickly after you put the book down. (A good follow-up question for all the people who gave it four stars on Amazon: Are you a millionaire?)

The book is divided into two sections, one for right-brained readers and the other for left-brained readers. The right-brained section tells the story of a fictional waitress who achieves her goal of millionaire status in a month. All she has to do was fortuitously meet a highly successful and wealthy business women and badger her into taking an interest in a waitress's plight and then convince all of her friends to tirelessly work for free in order to make her rich. Sounds easy, right? The left-brained, practical, section primarily focuses on taking advantage of the housing bubble and buying up properties and flipping them for a fast profit. The constant mantra is to pick the worst house in the best neighborhood.

This may be good advice for flipping houses during a housing bubble. And if you have a time machine, I say go for it. If your goal is to live somewhere that will be good for your mental well-being, you may want to take a different approach. Pick the best house in the worst neighborhood. We measure our level of success not in absolute terms, but in comparison with those around us. If you have the only ranch house on a street of McMansions then you're going to feel like the ugly step sister. On the other hand, if you have a tricked out double-wide in a row of single-width trailers, you're the big man in the trailer park. Sweet!

Jeff Yeager, the self-described "Ultimate Cheapskate," suggests that most people spend so much time thinking about the resale value of their home that they gear their improvement projects on pleasing the *next guy*. Rather than enjoying the home they are living in and creating a space that is all about expressing themselves, they are constantly anticipating the next move.

"Finishing in a starter home affords you one of life's greatest luxuries," he wrote, "one that most house climbers never get to experience, despite their apparent residential riches. I'm talking about the luxury of being able to make your house your home."

Besides, mansions are an environmental nightmare. If you had one, you would probably want your mansion to be beautifully appointed with rich woods—walnut, rosewood, and ebony, which are chopped out of old-growth forests and rainforests. Although many countries place restrictions on logging in old-growth forests, there is little meaningful enforcement. For timber barons, the benefit of illegal logging far outweighs the nearly non-existent penalties.

The Tanjung Putting National Park in Borneo has been disappearing one tree at a time as illegal loggers cut down rare species and process them in sawmills located *right in the park*. The practice is threatening the habitat of rare orangutans. Indonesia's largest environmental group, Walhi, claims that 85 percent of flooding and landslides in the country are caused by illegal logging.

Human Rights Watch released a report in January 2002 that said Sumatra has "wreaked havoc" on the environment and the human rights of Sumatra's indigenous people over the past twenty years by engaging in "rampant deforestation." A November 2003 flash flood, which caused a hillside to crash down on a village and resulted in the deaths of more than two hundred people, was blamed on deforestation.

The demand for mahogany has nearly wiped out the Caribbean's mahogany trees. Haiti has been particularly plundered. More than 90 percent of the country is now deforested. In Peru, loggers earn about $7 a day hacking away at the rainforest under dangerous conditions. The World Resources Institute reports that four-fifths of the world's original forest cover has been lost or degraded by human activity, and according to the Rainforest Action Network, tropical rainforests the size of two football fields disappear in the world every second. In the United States a mahogany tree can be made into about fifteen dining tables, which each might retail for as much as $120,000. It's a losing battle.

And have you given any thought to how many chemicals you would release into the environment to maintain that lush, weed-free lawn? The lawn is a relatively recent invention. It began as a status symbol of wealthy Europeans who used them to show they had so much land, they didn't even have to grow crops on all of it.

"A lawn is continually being altered by humans; ecologically speaking, it's a permanent catastrophe, exactly like the wheel ruts on the prairie," wrote Anita Sanchez, author of *The Teeth of the Lion*. "The native protecting vegetation has been stripped aside, the natural rhythm of succession altered. Healing can never take place. Long before the grass can grow tall to shade out the feral species, the mower roars across the landscape, cutting plants back to the ground."

Even a more modest suburban landscape has its perils. The suburbs are the manifestation of our dream to have a little place of our own in the country. As people follow the narrative of the lone cowboy riding into the sunset, or at least out of the city center, they abandon existing neighborhoods and enforce long commutes. They bulldoze the pines to create the Pine Knoll subdivision and fill it with rows of houses that are all the same. "The resulting environment is inevitably unstatisfying," wrote the authors of *Suburban Nation*, "its objective [is] self-contradictory: isolation en masse."

Take Me to Another Place, Take Me to Another Land

A few years ago, the residents of Osceola, Florida, approved a $29 million highway beautification project. When the county started planting trees along the roadside, the billboard industry's lobbyists intervened. They convinced the legislature to pass a bill granting billboards the right to a 500-foot-long uninterrupted view zone. Former state representative Randy Johnson told NPR, "Tourism depends on billboards, not trees."

In his book *The Geography of Nowhere*, James Howard Kunstler argues that our taste for suburban sprawl has wreaked havoc on community life. As the idea of land as a social resource morphed into the concept of land as real estate, "Other Old World values toppled before this novel system—for example, the idea of land as the physical container for community values. Nearly eradicated in the rush to profit was the concept of stewardship, of the land as a public trust."

There are many reasons to dislike big box stores—labor practices, their impact on the environment, undercutting prices of mom-and-pop stores and driving them out of business—but the best reason to dislike them, in my opinion, is their complete lack of aesthetics. We admire cultures of the past who built great edifices, chapels and pyramids to invoke inspiration and awe. Big box stores represent an America that is utterly artless. Giant fluorescent-lit warehouses with

212 BROKE IS BEAUTIFUL

rows and rows of stuff are a symbol of an America that sees no value in anything that cannot be bought or sold. Spend money on branding, perhaps, but not on beauty. Live in the suburban sprawl and this is your environment.

Have you ever driven through the mountains? You may have noticed that some of the most breathtaking scenery in the nation seems to be paradoxically reserved for the poorest people. Clinging to the side of many a mountain you will see run-down shacks with rusted out cars parked alongside. From such modest dwellings you can see for miles across a natural wonder that is almost transcendent in its beauty. Why do the broke get such a view to themselves? Because mountains are one of the last places where you can't build large factories or strip malls. We can put farms on the flat land, but we have yet to come up with many ways to draw profit from them thar' hills. (Except for blasting and mining them for minerals.) So who has the better deal, the rich person in a gated community full of identical giant mini-mansions, or the guy with a quiet life and a clear view of God's creation? Almost heaven, West Virginia . . .

———————◆———————

When the British author G. K. Chesterton was visiting New York he was taken to Times Square, where he gazed at the cascade of flashing neon advertisements. Chesterton remarked: "How beautiful it would be for someone who cannot read."

———————◆———————

What's in Your Wallet?

One night a burglar broke into the French author Honore de Balzac's single-room apartment and tried to pick the lock on the writer's desk. The bad guy was startled by a sardonic laugh from the bed, where Balzac, who he had supposed was asleep, lay watching him. "Why are you laughing?" asked the thief. "I am laughing to think what risks you take to try to find money in a desk by night where the legal owner can never find any by day."

29

You're Not Broke, You're Spiritually Evolved

"Nothing that is God's is obtainable by money."

—TERTULLIAN, CARTHAGINIAN THEOLOGICAL WRITER

My father's favorite story was of a Buddhist monk who had only one possession in life, his wooden bowl. The monk went from door to door and begged for pennies to put into his bowl. Then he bought rice with those pennies, which he ate from the bowl with his fingers. Next he washed the bowl, and filled it with water to drink. One day our monk was at the stream washing his only possession when it slipped from his hands. It fell on a rock and broke apart. He looked down at the broken bowl in astonishment. Then he looked up at heaven and said, "Free at last!"

Contrast that story with the following real headline from 2008: "Financial Woes Force Church to Sell Private Jet." The church in question preached the "Prosperity Gospel." Prosperity churches are based on the idea that success in business or personal life is evidence of God's love.

No word on whether they were planning on using the private jet to get a camel through the eye of a needle.

Americans put "In God We Trust" on the money to demonstrate that money is not God. But if people were not confusing money with God to begin with, there would be no need to print it there. Perhaps it is time to reframe your priorities.

Saddled with the stigma of being broke? Let's pause to ponder the origin of the word *stigma*. *Stigma* comes from the Latin, and it means a blot or blemish. During the heyday of their empire, the merciful Romans literally *branded* undesirables. The process left behind a physical *stigma*. Many of the undesirables they branded were Christians. The Christians took what was meant to be a mark of shame and held it up as a symbol of the nail wounds of Christ, which came to be known as the *stigmata*.

"Here is a rare example of not just a backward application (metalepsis) but a total reversal of meaning (antagonym)," wrote James B. Twitchell author of *Branded Nation*. "For the wounds received by Christ on the Cross would miraculously appear on the hands of a true penitent: the secondary stigmata, a brand of elevation, not degradation."

If the religious people of the past could manage to transform their social stigma into a virtue in a time when they were literally being fed to the lions, how much easier is it for you to transform your financial stigma into a virtue?

Think there are no poor heroes to emulate? How about Mahatma Gandhi, Mother Theresa, Jesus Christ? For centuries, people have taken a principled stand against materialism in the name of religious observance. They felt that abandoning the pursuit of property allowed them a greater focus on God and the eternal soul, and that is something no repo man can take from you.

The ancient Chinese philosopher Confucius said, "The mind of the superior man is conversant with righteousness; the mind of the mean man is conversant with gain." Confucius believed in a philosophy called *xiaokang*, which literally means being moderately well-off. To achieve harmony, each household has its material needs met. They are less than affluent, but better than in need. With people living lives of moderation, material needs are available to be distributed equitably to all.

Ancient Jewish economic policy held that all wealth was, to paraphrase Rush Limbaugh, "on loan from God." This was a lesson that was illustrated in the seventh-year Shabbat, a sabbatical in which the land was allowed to rest and the Jewish people had to trust that God would provide. During the seventh-year Shabbat (the word means "pausing" or "ceasing" in Hebrew) debts were forgiven, and each man was expected to study the Torah and give thanks for life. During the fiftieth-year Jubilee the original land allocated under Moses to each individual tribe was redistributed. This was to prevent the accumulation of land by small monopolies. It also required people to give up their attachments.

Jesus, in the words of Christian historian Ray Petrie, "had not even a place to lay his head. He ended on the cross a career of self-abnegation, which was as total as it was unselfish. He renounced his own will and his own life for others in liberating poverty of spirit."

Blessed are the poor, for yours is the Kingdom of God.

—LUKE 6:20

Why not shuck off the mantle of failed capitalism, and try on the cloak of the great spiritual renunciates throughout the ages, who believed in the cleansing value of total and redemptive poverty.

"The vow of poverty," wrote John Lord in the 1885 *Beacon Lights of History*, "was a stern, lofty, disdainful protest against the most dangerous and demoralizing evil of the [Roman] Empire. It hurled scorn, hatred, and defiance on this overwhelming evil and invoked the aid of Christianity. It was simply the earnest affirmation and belief that money could not buy the higher joys of earth, and might jeopardize the hopes of heaven."

The prosperity gospel and churches that have a fleet of private jets are quite at odds with traditional Christianity, argues James B. McDaniel in his book, *Living from the Center*. Consumerism is about striving after material goods. Christianity is about freedom from attachments.

Christianity, he wrote, "is a religion of freedom from clinging and freedom for love. Sometimes it can seem as if these two are opposites, as if freedom from clinging and freedom for love are at odds with each other. But in truth they go together. The freer we are from holding on to things as if they were private possessions, the freer we are to love our neighbors on their own terms and for their own sakes and to love God in a similar way. The heart of Christianity is a letting-go-into-love."

For the past few years I have been traveling throughout the country with a Russian ballet dancer to bring classical ballet master classes to students from New York to Florida to Iowa. We travel in my car along highways and interstates. As we ride, it is impossible to escape the fact that in spite of all predictions to the contrary, religion is alive and well in America. It appears in uniquely American forms like the Christian rock we encounter on the radio, the billboards advertising Jesus, and the giant crosses that spring up along the highways. One of the most obtrusive can be found on I-75 in Tennessee just before passing into Kentucky. A giant "Adult World" superstore sits curiously beside an even more gigantic white cross. It stands 101 feet, 6 inches from the ground and appears to be made out of aluminum siding.

James Potter, the preacher who planted the large cross, said, "You know the Bible tells us to stir up their spirit. Well there's no way you can do it except something big, you know."

In his book *Travels with Charlie*, John Steinbeck speculates that because people have nothing to look at on superhighways they are forced to daydream. He believed that the superhighways would have the effect of making people more self-absorbed. But enough about him . . .

I believe superhighways have an opposite effect. They have made us more extroverted. We have to shout louder. On a two-lane highway, you see every fruit vendor and every old woman weaving sweetgrass baskets at a South Carolina roadside stand. You're traveling at a pace at which you can take in the eccentric little diners and dinosaur-themed miniature golf courses. From a side road you can see steeples and quietly welcoming rural churches.

"Maybe such subtelty worked when there were no highways," wrote James B. Twitchell in *Shopping for God*, "but no longer. The steeple showed only that the building was a church, not which denomination or 'flavor' of church." Thus the invention of the church sign, modeled after movie theater marquees. Church signs could try to express the variety of religious life inside to busy people rushing by.

The first church signs in the United States were stationed outside traditional steepled edifices. But the more mobile the people, the more the churches relied on other types of communication to get the word out. Yellow page ads, giant billboards, televangelism. The more they relied on other forms of communication to define what was inside, the less important the facade. And so the little old steepeled church, expensive to build and maintain, was replaced by the more ordinary building. A church could be in a big, beige block of a building or a storefront or a warehouse. What makes it a church is not the artistry of its structure, but its interior life. It makes us choice-rich but architecture-poor.

(My favorite church sign message so far? "Even when you don't sneeze.")

In America, we have a smorgasboard of religions, and even though many people remain in the religion they were brought up in, we are always aware of the opportunity for change. We are handed cards inviting us to new churches when we come out of the shopping center. Jehovah's witnesses come to our door. The Unitarian church runs underwriting messages on NPR. We make a choice to stay with the familiar or to change.

Russia, with its one church, doesn't have this marketing problem. You don't need a sign to explain what variety of religious experience awaits you. You know exactly what will happen inside. It is the same for most countries in Europe. When I was an exchange student in high school I discovered that most French people (the growing Muslim population notwithstanding) are Roman Catholic by default. If you're

Russian you're orthodox, whether you attend church or not. There is little to no "church shopping," thus no church signs or giant billboards of Jesus. The grand edifices of European cathedrals remain as sublime symbols of a culture larger than the individual. What makes them sublime? Philosopher Edmund Burke argued that landscapes were "sublime" if they produced a feeling of weakness.

Wrote Alain de Botton in *The Art of Travel*, "Sublime places embodied a defiance to man's will. . . . Sublime places repeat in grand terms a lesson that ordinary life typically introduces viciously: that the universe is mightier than we are, that we are frail and temporary and have no alternative but to accept limitations on our will; that we must bow to necessities greater than ourselves."

Many U.S. religions are more focused on "elevating" and "uplifting" than making us humbled and small. If you have free choice, after all, you're much more likely to choose a church that tells you you're the best. That feels pretty good. If we're already inclined to believe that wealth and success go to the hardest working and most ethical among us, then we will be attracted to doctrines that reinforce that belief. God wants you to be rich! It is a bit hard to come away with that view from reading the red letters in the King James Bible though.

Jesus said, "Blessed are the meek, for the meek shall inherit the earth." (To which comedian A. Whitney Brown added: "We'll just take it back from them. What are they going to do? They're a bunch of meeks.")

I have always interpreted this line to mean that the meek would triumph in a future world and would eventually rule. This is the "elevating" and "uplifting" religious approach. But I have started to wonder if he might have meant something all together different.

The meek are the anonymous. They inherit the earth one grave stone at a time. They give their bodies to the soil and leave their names not on monuments but in dusty archives as records of births and deaths. The meek inherit the earth by becoming the earth. In our smallness we are the same, we are keepers of the earth and kept by the earth. The small inhabit the earth together.

Factoid: Seventy percent of Americans visit malls each week, more than attend houses of worship.

30

It's Hard Out There for the Rich— or, Money Can't Buy Happiness

....

Hamlet: My excellent good friends! How dost thou, Guilden-stern? Ah, Rosencrantz! Good lads, how do ye both?

Rosencrantz: As the indifferent children of the earth.

Guildenstern: Happy, in that we are not over-happy, on fortune's cap we are not the very button.

—WILLIAM SHAKESPEARE, *HAMLET*

Money can't buy happiness. I know what you're saying: "Give me $1 million and I'll be happy to test the hypothesis." But hear me out.

It's true that money can make you happy, up to a point. When money is the difference between living in a cardboard box or a clean apartment, between having medical care or going without, it makes a person more comfortable and satisfied. But when money is the difference between a good car and a luxury car, a 4 GB MP3 player or a 120 GB MP3 player, this year's computer or last year's, its ability to bring joy falls off sharply. Economists call this "declining marginal utility."

"Many psychological studies have shown that materialism is associated not with happiness, but with dissatisfaction, depression, anxiety, anger, isolation, and alienation," wrote researcher Richard Eckersley. "Human needs for security and safety, competence and self-worth, connectedness to others, and autonomy and authenticity are relatively unsatisfied when materialistic values predominate."

There is a scene in *Star Wars* where Luke Skywalker tries to convince Han Solo to rescue Princess Leia. He tells Solo that if he rescues her he will have more wealth than he can imagine. "I don't know," he answers. "I can *imagine* quite a bit." Whatever sum he is rewarded for saving the universe, it is probably not going to be enough to satisfy Han Solo.

Researchers have found that when people find it easy to imagine an event, they overestimate the likelihood that it will actually occur. The easier it is for Han Solo to envision becoming filthy rich, the less likely it is that he'll be pleased if he only gets a little bit grubby.

The more money you have, the higher your expectations, and the more you expect, the more you're likely to find your life wanting in comparison. Our level of dissatisfaction, it turns out, comes not from what we have but the gulf between what our lives are like and what we think they should be like.

A recent poll of New Yorkers found that people who earned more than $200,000 a year were likelier than those in any other income group to feel poor when seeing other people with money. Inherited-wealth expert John L. Levy coined the term "bag-lady syndrome" to describe the panic of wealthy people when they imagine losing their money. They don't think they could possibly survive. If riches make us happy, why does Japan, one of the richest countries in the world, also have one of the highest suicide rates?

To answer that, let's go back to Han Solo. We left him on the Millenium Falcon "imagining" large sums of money. Let's suppose that his dreams actually come true. Let's assume for the sake of argument that Princess Leia hands him the keys to the space vault and lets our pilot remove more wealth than even his advanced imagination could conjure. Surely he's happy now?

Nope. Here's why. When we imagine what is going to happen, we don't usually bother to imagine what else is going to happen, nor do we imagine what is *not* going to happen.

Han Solo may have had a vivid mental picture of himself as a wealthy star pilot. His fantasy probably included a brand-new spaceship, complete freedom and leisure, and getting the girl. He did not imagine that being the richest guy on Corellia would go to his head and that Princess Leia would run off with a handsome and uncomplicated droid. He did not imagine that he would be diagnosed with a rare version of the galactic flu and would be confined to a hospital without any opportunity to spend his riches. In fact, while he could imagine quite a bit, he probably didn't imagine his life continuing in any detail at all. He just assumed having the money would feel pretty good. Getting what you wanted and discovering that you still have problems is a real downer. What do you have to aspire to now? When you were broke, at least you could imagine how great your life would be once you had money. Who's going to feel sympathy for you, now that you're rich? They imagine quite a bit about your wealth as well.

Happiness researchers tell us that we are built to be a little bit uncomfortable. It is in our DNA to be creative and to try new things and to aspire to new heights. If you are satisfied with what you have, there is not much reason to get out of bed and try anything new. To trick us into doing that, rewards must always remain just over the horizon. No matter how hard we pull the sled, we are always destined to be the swing dog— that's the one directly behind the lead dog in a dog sled team.

It turns out that progressing toward things and achieving goals make us happy. Once we have the thing we desired, we're not that bothered. That is the dirty little secret of "retail therapy." *Acquiring* a consumer product makes us happy for about five minutes. *Having* it does not keep us happy.

Having a lot of money lying about just gives you options, and options, contrary to popular belief, are bad. If you're dead broke and someone gives you a television set, it makes you very happy. Now imagine you're rich. You go to the store and you find dozens of television sets. You could buy the newest flat screen, the one that is the size of a movie screen. You could get the one with the built-in DVD player. You eventually choose the one that integrates into your home computer entertainment portal, but it has so many features you can't figure out how to use it. You start to regret your purchase and to think about the more basic model you should have bought in the first place.

But hey, you've got money, so you go back to the store and you buy a few more televisions and you set them up in a special viewing room. Even that is not as good, somehow, as you imagined it would be. After the first day of watching three programs at once and playing with the Wii while listening to the Black-Eyed Peas, it gets a bit old. You end up like Elvis Presley in Graceland, shooting up screens when you dislike a show, out of sheer boredom. Next thing you know you're wearing a custom-made jumpsuit, taking too many drugs, and sweating a lot. You've started down a slippery slope toward ruin.

Have you ever stopped to think about this whole "pursuit of happiness" thing? Maybe pursuing happiness isn't all it's cracked up to be. From the beginning, America's inalienable right to the "pursuit of happiness" was tied to property.

In his *Second Treatise of Civil Government*, John Locke, the British philosopher, not the character on *Lost*, claimed that everyone has a right to "life, liberty, and property." This statement lies behind the famous sentence in our declaration. This covert connection between happiness and property confirms what Benjamin Franklin proposed throughout his work: The true road to earthly joy is through the accumulation of stuff.

Since we're supposed to be self-made, and our stuff is supposed to make us happy, we all go around with foolish grins on our faces lest we admit we might be failing.

Feeling Depressed? Enjoy the Pastime of the Great Depression

It was the 1930s, jobs were scarce, people whistled "Buddy Can You Spare a Dime" as they waited in bread lines, construction was virtually at a standstill, crop prices fell, manufacturing nearly ground to a halt. Yet one industry was pulling in profits of more than $225 million. What was it? Miniature golf. Dreamers were putting at (tiny) windmills from coast to coast. At its peak the country had some forty thousand miniature golf courses. (Now there are about sixteen hundred.) There was a running joke during the Depression that the only industry that was hiring was minigolf, an inexpensive game said to "cure Depression blues." The players often putted with abandon until dawn, causing many cities to enforce "Blue Laws" against the little sport.

Back when I was a theater student, one of my instructors opened his class by asking: "Does anyone here have an inferiority complex?" The room was silent. I wanted to raise my hand and say, "Yes . . . well, that is, I sort of have an inferiority complex, but it's not a very good one." But because this was the truth, I did not.

Today, thanks to our intensive self-esteem indoctrination in school and on TV, we all know that a sense of self-worth is probably the most important thing a person can possess. We know that you can't love another unless you love yourself first. Ours is a culture that changed "And the winner is . . ." to "And the Oscar goes to . . ." to avoid hurting the feelings of movie stars by implying they may not entirely have won. (Meryl Streep, what a loser!)

We know that those with high self-esteem go far and those with low self-esteem do not. (And that going far is important.) We know that if you can dream it you can be it. We know all of these things because we have been taught them over and over on television talk shows, in classrooms, and in song. But just because we *know* it doesn't mean it is true!

The problem with all this self-love is that most of the self-esteem programs and self-help manuals focus on feeling good about yourself for no particular reason. Your sense of self-worth is not tied to achievement, relationships, or community standards. Feeling good about yourself in this philosophy matters more than what you do.

The catch is that the real world does judge you by what you *do*, not by how you feel. When we discover this, we feel as though we've been sold a bill of goods. This sucks because it is really bad for our self-esteem, which, as you know, is the most important thing in life.

Enough time has passed for scholars to start assessing the outcomes of all of our self-esteem training. Not surprisingly, they found that there is only a small correlation between self-esteem and grades, and it is probably because kids feel better about themselves when they do well, not because feeling good makes them do better.

In fact, the California Task Force to Promote Self-Esteem and Personal and Social Responsibility, which spent a quarter of a million dollars to make California's students feel sunnier about life, found that self-esteem isn't linked to academic achievement, good behavior, or any of the goals the task force was created to address. Self-esteem doesn't protect against drug abuse, broken homes, welfare dependency, or juvenile delinquency.

"The enthusiastic claims of the self-esteem movement mostly range from fantasy to hogwash," wrote Dr. Roy Baumeister, a social psychologist from Princeton University. "The effects of self-esteem are small, limited, and not all good. My conclusion is that self-control is worth ten times as much as self-esteem."

The self-esteem indoctrination has had one clear effect, though. It has made a generation optimistic—almost insanely so. In a recent survey, 98 percent of college freshmen agreed with the statement, "I am sure that one day I will get to where I want to be in life."

They also believe that success will come quickly. Jean Twenge, author of *Generation* Me, wrote, "One of my students, who wasn't more than twenty-two, noted during a class presentation that 'there are lots of people our age who are CEOs of their own companies.' He probably read a profile or two of one of these rare beasts in a magazine and, fueled by the 'you can be anything' mythos, decided that this was commonplace."

In 1999, college freshmen predicted they would be earning, on average, $75,000 a year by the time they were thirty. This was at a time when the average salary of a thirty-year-old was $27,000.

Here's a handy word you may want to know: *cresomaniac*:—A person who suffers from delusions of wealth.

This cheerful generation ran up their credit cards in anticipation of their double-inflated salary expectations, bless their hearts. In 2008, 84 percent of college undergrads had at least one credit card. The average balance of undergraduate credit cards was $3,173 and the average senior now graduates with $4,100 in debt.

"Naturally—we didn't get paid, owing to circumstance ever so slightly beyond our control, and all the money we had we lost betting on certainties."

—"PLAYER" IN TOM STOPPARD'S ROSENCRANTZ AND GILDENSTERN ARE DEAD

The self-esteem generation's expectations are so sky high that, in Twenge's words, "we will probably get less of what we want than any previous generation."

Holocaust survivor Victor Frankl's *Man's Search for Meaning* drew on the experiences of concentration camp prisoners. He found that those who survived were not the ones who pursued happiness as an end in itself, but the ones who had a goal in life. Meaning—*not* pleasure—was the key. This can be a great comfort if you're facing hard times. It is much easier to find "meaning" in hard times than "happiness."

Jay McDaniel, a theologian and author of the book *Living from the Center*, calls happiness a "byproduct, not a goal": ". . . many people can live very meaningful lives," he wrote, "pursuing quite worthy goals, without being particularly happy, if 'happiness' means pleasant states of consciousness. Consider the person who is deeply compassionate, sharing in the sorrows of others, and who, precisely through her sharing, cannot sleep well at night. In her empathy for others, she knows the happiness of communion with others, but not the happiness of pleasure."

Would U.S. culture have been different if the authors of the Declaration of Independence had written, "We hold these truths to be self-evident, that all men are created equal, that they are endowed by their Creator with certain unalienable Rights, that among these are Life, Liberty, and the Pursuit of Meaning?"

It's worth thinking about.

I Want a New Drug

Pharmaceutical names are now carefully chosen by linguistic experts for how they resonate with consumers. Prozac was chosen because the p, z, and k sounds score highly for the qualities "active" and "daring." Paxil likewise contains k and z sounds and also has cracking, buzzing sounds, bringing electricity to the sequence "ac," which calls to mind "action." Zoloft takes the Greek *zo,* which means "life" and marries it to *loft,* which reminds us of elevation.

Sex Is Still Free!

"I regret to say that we of the FBI are powerless to act in cases of oral-genital intimacy, unless it has in some way obstructed interstate commerce."

—J. EDGAR HOOVER, FORMER FBI DIRECTOR

As a broke person, restaurants are off-limits. Gourmet meals are probably not a regular occurrence. The latest CD by your favorite band has been on your Amazon.com wish list for months. You can't afford a movie or a DVD rental. Rock concerts and Broadway shows are completely out of the question. Even the ice cream social at the fire house has a ticket price.

Yet one of the greatest pleasures of adult life is available to you absolutely free of charge. It requires no electricity, no batteries, no running water. You don't even need any clothing! (Those are optional extras of course, but not required.) Sex has no entry fee. Come one, come all, rich or poor!

One of the most interesting things about sex—feel free to debate me on this—is that our views on sexuality seem to have taken an opposite trajectory to our views on almost every other aspect of life. In an increasingly commercial society in which everything seems to have a price tag, sex is the last activity that we have not monetized. As we increasingly see our lives in marketplace terms, we make it illegal in most places to charge money for sex. It seems as though the more consumerism has pervaded our lives, the more marriage and sexuality have shucked off their bonds to economic social contracts.

The concept of romantic love as a reason for marriage, rather than marrying for financial and social status, is a very recent invention. Today we expect romantic love and sexual compatibility to be the main ingredients of a marriage. When they go, the marriage often goes, as witnessed by our high divorce rates.

Judge: What do you mean you want a divorce because you live in a two story house? What kind of a reason is that to ask for a divorce?

Petitioner: Well judge, The first story is "I've got a headache," and the second story is, "This is the wrong time of the month!"

This is a stunning turn around from the life that Edith Wharton describes in her 1905 novel *House of Mirth*.* The tragedy of the main character, Lily Bart, is not that she enters a loveless marriage for social advancement, but that she is unable to. She desires a love-match, and so sabotages all of her socially acceptable marriage options, and yet she is too bound by her culture to marry beneath what she envisions to be her station. This conflict eventually leads to her complete downfall. (It's not one of those happy, feel-good stories.)

Bart's societal expectations are summed up in this passage in which she banters comfortably with a male friend, Lawrence Selden.

---

* *In 1897, Edith Wharton published* The Decoration of Houses, *in which she argued that people should live modestly, and that it was unseemly to make a show of money. At the time she lived in a thirty-five-room mansion and was attended by ten full-time servants.*

The fact that Selden works for a living puts him below her social radar as marriage material.

"You don't know how much I need such a friend," she said. "... the other women—my best friends—well, they use me or abuse me; but they don't care a straw what happens to me. I've been about too long—people are getting tired of me; they are beginning to say I ought to marry."

There was a moment's pause, during which Selden meditated one or two replies calculated to add a momentary zest to the situation; but he rejected them in favour of the simple question: "Well, why don't you? ... Isn't marriage your vocation? Isn't it what you're all brought up for?"

She sighed. "I suppose so. What else is there?"

... She shook her head wearily. "I threw away one or two good chances when I first came out—I suppose every girl does; and you know I am horribly poor—and very expensive. I must have a great deal of money ..."

"What's become of Dillworth?" he asked.

"Oh, his mother was frightened—she was afraid I should have all the family jewels reset. And she wanted me to promise that I wouldn't do over the drawing-room."

"The very thing you are marrying for!"

"Exactly. So she packed him off to India."

We now call someone who trades sex for social status a gold digger, and we find it distasteful. We have come to firmly believe that a marriage should be based on romantic love and sexual attraction. A generation that came of age after women's lib and the pill views co-habitation and pre-marital sex as natural and normal. Gay marriage could only become an issue in an era that defines marriage as primarily a love-match. For the most part we are marrying and having sex for love and lust, a triumph of emotions over economics.

Regardless of what Marilyn Monroe may have said, diamonds are not a girl's best friend. Her best friend is the G-spot. Dartmouth College economist David Blachflower and University of Warwick (England) professor Andrew Oswald found that sex made people happier than money. After evaluating the levels of sexual activity and happiness in sixteen thousand people, they found that sex so positively influenced happiness that they estimated increasing intercourse from once a month to once a week is equivalent to the happiness generated by getting a $50,000 raise. And in case you were wondering, people who make more money do not have more sex. Nor, as is sometimes assumed, do the poor have more sex. There was no difference in the study between sexual frequency and income levels.

Not only is sex fun, it is good for you. Various studies show it can relieve stress and help you sleep, and it can have an anti-depressant effect. It gives you an immune system boost. Dr. Dudley Chapman, a gynecologist, says orgasms boost infection fighting-cells up to 20 percent. Psychologists at Wilkes University in Pennsylvania found that students who had regular sexual activity had a third higher level of an antibody that fights colds and flu. A study from the Advanced Institute of Human Sexuality looked at the sex lives of ninety thousand adults and discovered that sexually active people took fewer sick days.

A series of studies have found that women who have sex regularly have more regular menstrual cycles. Frequent sexual activity may increase fertility, reduce PMS symptoms, and relieve menstrual cramps. Women who have frequent sex have higher levels of estrogen in their systems, which has been linked to cardiovascular health, lower bad cholesterol, and increased bone density. A 1989 study suggested that increased frequency of sexual activity was linked to a reduced risk of breast cancer.

It's not bad for men either: Studies have suggested that more frequent ejaculation can help prevent chronic infections of the prostate. An Australian study suggests frequent ejaculation may reduce the risk of prostate cancer. Increased testosterone released by sexual activity can help strengthen bones and muscles and has been linked to heart health and a reduced risk of Alzheimer's disease.

Sex boosts the production of the hormone DHEA, which has been linked to improved brain function. Orgasms can relieve pain associated with migraine headaches and arthritis.

You may not be able to afford health insurance, but hey, you can still call that special someone and arrange a rendez-vous. Free love, baby! Make love, not money! Go for it.

Handy Household Hint: That time of the month and not enough change to buy your favorite brand of sanitary product? Do what your great-grandmothers did. Spend a week on the rag. Before disposables, women used layers of rags, which they washed out and reused. Some crunchy granola women are going this route for ecological reasons. Be sure to use multiple layers. It is more absorbent than a single thick rag.

32

Luxury Goods Ain't What They Used to Be

"Unless you have a feeling for that secret knowledge that modest things can be more beautiful than anything expensive, you will never have style."

—ANDRÉE PUTMAN, PARISIAN INTERIOR DECORATOR

There are some perfectly good reasons you wouldn't want luxury goods anyway. Redefine your lack of these signs of opulence as political awareness, and you'll feel much better. For the most part, when you're buying an upscale brand, you're just asking for permission to pay extra money.

One of the greatest examples has to be the "designer jeans" craze of the 1980s. Denim trousers came into existence as clothes for miners, and they were the quintessential working man's outfit, a decidedly low-class affair, and later a rustic sign of down-scale teen culture. That was until a pair of Israeli-born, New York garment makers named Nakash invented "Jordache." It sounds like the name of a French fashion designer, and that's the idea. Voila! upscale jeans for the fashion-conscious with a suitable, exotic, French-sounding name. The idea took off—by 1979, there were thirty different companies making designer jeans, and you were wearing Anderson Cooper's mom's name on your butt. (You knew he was Gloria Vanderbilt's kid, right?) At the height of the designer jeans craze, Americans were buying sixty thousand pairs an hour. The industry was turning out 500,000 miles of jeans a year—enough fabric to span the equator twenty times.

Of course, Jordache was not the first faux foreign product aimed at U.S. consumers. *The New York* Times even coined a term for the practice: "the Vichyssoise Strategy." Vichyssoise, cold potato soup, was created at the Ritz Carlton hotel in New York. To make it palatable to the American diner, it was named in mock French. Häagen Dazs ice cream was invented in the Bronx in 1960. A Polish immigrant, Reuben Mattus, concocted the Scandinavian sounding name and put a map of Denmark on the carton. Häagen Dazs means nothing in Danish. In English it means "overpriced."

In the 1970s, Chrysler's luxury Cordoba had television advertisements featuring actor Ricardo Montalban boasting about the vehicle's "Corinthian leather" seats. The leather did not come from the Greek city of Corinth, or anywhere else in Europe for that matter. Advertising executives made the term up. The leather reportedly came from exotic New Jersey.

Thanks to re-branding, the Chilean sea bass, which for starters is not necessarily from Chile and is not a bass (its original and less appetizing name was the Patagonian toothfish), has been seriously overfished. The toothfish was described by NPR as "a very ugly fish with big bulging eyes and little pointy teeth which, nonetheless, became the darling of high-end restaurants and their foodie customers." It's all in the name really. As the Chilean sea bass it commands prices of more than $22 a pound.

There are far more compelling ethical reasons than not being a marketing dupe to opt out of "champagne wishes and caviar dreams." Luxurious beluga caviar, which sells for about $240 an ounce, was so overfished that the United States was finally forced to ban its import in 2005. Stocks had declined more than 90 percent over the previous twenty years. That bluefin tuna used in swanky sushi is being overfished to near extinction.

Bruce Knecht, author of *Hooked: Pirates, Poaching, and the Perfect Fish* told NPR, "We have explored pretty much everywhere when it comes to fish, and it seems highly unlikely to me—and, of course, the scientists that I've talked to—that we're going to find a fish that's both attractive to humans and exists in large numbers that we haven't come across before. We really are at the end of the line."

Envious of those who sip Evian? It's really not much of an improvement over Eau de Tap. And bottled water comes with its own moral hazards. The bottles are a major contributor to global warming. Last year, Americans consumed 8.3 billion gallons of bottled water, about 27.6 gallons per person. Making all those bottles produces more than 2.5 million tons of CO_2. The energy required to make one plastic liter bottle, fill it with water from a spring in the Sierra Nevada, truck it to San Jose, and then bury the empty in a landfill creates about as much CO as an average car emits driving a quarter of a mile. Now imagine the impact of those bottles flown in from France and Fiji.

Feeling sorry for yourself for driving a "previously-owned" 1984 Chevy Citation? Don't be. Alexander Karas, owner of a Rolls-Royce limousine service in Baltimore once called the Rolls "a piece of crap." He pointed out that the Rolls-Royce constantly needs to be oiled and just as constantly breaks down.

"You almost need a mechanic with you in the trunk," he said. "It's the biggest marketing scam in history.... The new ones are not hand built—they're spot welded, and the drive train they now use is the same one that Disney uses in the antique cars in the Magic Kingdom. It's a marketing con job, but Rolls-Royce is a name, and they're riding on it."

Which is good, because they are not riding on their own automatic transmission, Karas says. From 1955–1965 they used the General Motors hydromatic, the same thing you'd find in a Buick, Oldsmobile, or Cadillac. In 1966, they switched to the Chrysler Torque-Flight transmission, which they still use. They get their air conditioner from General Motors. The shocks come from a company in France.

Rocky H. Aoki, head of the Benihana chain of Japanese steak houses, was once quoted as saying about a Rolls he bought from the Sheik of Bahrain: "Very unreliable car. Very costly to maintain.... Engine blew up."

But in spite of this, Aoki is still a fan of the car. "I like the style of the Rolls," he said. "I don't care about engine. Big car, really eye-catching."

I guess if you are choosing between exploding cars and money is no object, you might be inclined to take the Rolls over the Ford Pinto. If you prefer your car to actually go, you're probably better off with what you've got.

Factoid: In 1991, during another rough patch for the economy, a new men's cologne was introduced. The fragrance was called Recession, and it was billed as an "Owe de Cologne" for "the man who used to have everything." It's slogan was: "The economy stinks, you shouldn't have to." *Parade* magazine, in its "Best and Worst" issue hailed it as the year's best new product.

33

How to Eat III: Gardening and Foraging

....

"It is pleasanter to eat one's own peas out of one's garden, than to buy them by the peck at Covent Garden."

—CHARLES LAMB, ENGLISH ESSAYIST

Getting fed shouldn't be too much of a problem because food really does grow on trees. Depending on your region of the country or the world you can go no farther than your front yard to find apple trees, avocado trees, or raspberry bushes. With a little pre-planning and the willingness to get your hands dirty, your summer garden can yield more tomatoes, cucumbers, and lettuce than you can possibly eat yourself. As the old joke says, you eat what you can and what you can't, you can. Or freeze. There is really only one key to cooking in bulk and freezing the left-overs: label what you put in the freezer.

Even if you're too much of a type-A personality to plant seeds and wait for sprouts to poke out of the soil, nature will provide. Growing like weeds are many edible plant species from wild leeks to nettles to violets and all sorts of berries.

One of my fondest memories is going mushroom hunting in a Massachusetts park with a Russian friend. (I have not met a Russian who does not consider mushroom hunting to be one of life's great pleasures.) I left the species identification up to my friend, and in retrospect, I may have been a bit too trusting that someone raised in another country would be an expert in local mushrooms. Fortunately, we spent a pleasant afternoon plucking up fungus and putting it in pails. I enjoyed the whole experience so much that I completely forgot I do not like mushrooms. We ate the fruits of our labors and didn't die, so I'm still here to recommend this activity to you, especially if you actually like mushrooms. One caveat: You have to know what you're doing because some mushrooms are poisonous, but there are many guides to help you out. Look them up in your local library.

"Wildman" Steve Brill's guide to foraging (www.wildmanstevebrill.com) contains recipes for such dishes as wild-carrot onion soup, violet flower sherbert, and pokeweed baked eggs, along with tips for identifying edible species. Or you can pick up a field guide to edible wild plants. Remember that some plants, like Queen Anne's lace, aka wild carrot, are edible, but they have poisonous look-alikes. Queen Anne's lace can be easily confused with hemlock. Because I am not personally an expert in the subject, and I hold it as a badge of honor that I have never poisoned one my readers, I am going to stick to the story of one edible wild plant I am fairly sure both you and I can identify: the dandelion.

Besides being an important tool for gauging whether or not you like butter when you hold it under your chin, the dandelion is a highly nutritious herb originally transported to the United States by European settlers who prized its medicinal properties. The botanical name for the dandelion *Taraxacum officinale* loosely translates to "official remedy for disorders." Every part of the herb—its leaves, flowers, stem, and roots—was used, providing remedies for indigestion, aches and pains, insomnia, and minor cuts and scrapes. They made their way west with the wagon trains. The pioneers purposely planted them as garden flowers. As they became increasingly popular as a food crop, horticulturalists developed numerous tasty varieties. French large-leaved dandelions were served in the best restaurants in Paris.

As our love for lush green lawns overtook our need for home-grown medicinal gardens, we stopped cultivating dandelions. Fortunately, the crafty dandelions escaped using the clever trick of convincing small children their wishes would come true if they blew away the white puff ball of seeds. Now it is nearly impossible to get rid of them. A large percentage of the estimated forty billion dollars we spend each year on lawn care is mobilized in a futile attempt to eradicate the once-valued comestible. I mention this by way of warning. If you decide to pluck some yellow buds to fry up a tasty dandelion omelet, be sure you're not foraging in a lawn that has been sprayed by TruGreen.

The easiest, and arguably the most satisfying, way to eat the stuff is to toss the leaves into a salad. The greens can also be boiled like spinach or infused to make tea. And of course there is dandelion wine. To make this time-honored beverage, pick the flowers at noon when they are open wide, then clean them and boil them with sugar and orange peel, pour the mixture into glass bottles, and set them aside for several months until they ferment. The result is a sweet, yellow sparkling beverage that probably will never displace Chardonnay, but it's pleasing enough for a drink you made all by yourself. You can speed up the process a bit by adding yeast. Various combinations and techniques can easily be found on the Internet.

Even if the humble dandelion does not become your favorite comfort food, it is just about the most nutrient-rich snack you'll ever pluck from your lawn. It contains protein and carbohydrates and is low in calories. I'm told one cup of cooked dandelion greens contains 10,000 IUs of vitamin A, 147 mg of calcium, 244 mg of potassium, 203 mg of vitamin K, and 3 g of fiber. It's also a rich source of beta-carotene.

Need more advice on foraging, growing, and sustainable eating? Great news: *The Whole Earth Catalog* has just put all its back issues online. You can read them—for free! There's a happy hippie soy farmer in you somewhere. Celebrate him!

THINGS TO BE THANKFUL FOR

You've probably never been driven out of business by a company that bears your own name. That's what happened to Richard and Maurice McDonald. They opened a first-of-its-kind fast food shop in San Bernadino, California, shortly after World War II. When they sold it to a milkshake-machine salesman named Ray Kroc in 1961 for $2.7 million they gave up the right to use their own last name. "I needed the McDonald name and those golden arches," Kroc later said. "What are you going to do with a name like Kroc?"

The real McDonalds, however, had a bit of an attachment to the business they founded and built, and they insisted on keeping their flagship restaurant in San Bernadino. Since they couldn't use their

own name they dubbed it "Mac's Place." The McDonalds had no idea what they were up against.

"It's ridiculous to call this an industry," Kroc once said of the hamburger biz. "This is not. This is rat eat rat, dog eat dog. I'll kill 'em, and I'm going to kill 'em before they kill me. You're talking about the American way of survival of the fittest."

Kroc put a McDonald's across the street, and McDonald's put the McDonalds out of business.

34

If You Like It Should You Really Put a Ring on It?—Or, Reasons to Be Glad You Can't Afford a Diamond Ring

"Diamonds are forever, but tattoos are real commitment."

—GERALDO RIVERA, TELEVISION JOURNALIST

You've heard of blood diamonds, right? Blood diamonds, also known as conflict diamonds, come from war-torn African countries such as Angola, Sierra Leone and the Democratic Republic of Congo. Money from the export and sale of diamonds has been used to fuel violent civil wars. Notably war in Angola, in which thousands had their limbs hacked off and 500,000 people died.

In 2002, the United Nation tried to stem the tide of conflict diamonds by approving something called Kimberley Process Certification. It required participating countries to ensure that the sale of any diamond originating from the country does not fund a rebel group, that each diamond export is accompanied by a certificate, and that no diamond has been exported to or imported from a country that does not participate in the process.

The process has lowered the number of conflict diamonds in circulation, but there are problems with it. First of all, it is voluntary, which means it isn't always enforced. Also, the process only bans diamonds from countries that are in a state of civil war as defined by the United Nations. Simply allowing humanitarian atrocities like forced child labor and the occasional mutilation doesn't count. And then there are the ecological hazards. Diamonds come from open-pit mines, which cause erosion, water pollution, and habitat loss.

If all that talk of limb hacking and environment poisoning doesn't put you off, stop for a moment to ponder why you want a diamond in the first place. Diamonds, it turns out, are not all that rare. They are simply crystallized carbon, a first cousin to the graphite found in your "lead" pencil. In 2006, more than 75,000 pounds of diamonds were produced worldwide.

"A diamond is a precious commodity because everyone thinks it's a precious commodity," wrote Ulrich Boser in *Smithsonian*, "the geological equivalent of a bouquet of red roses, elegant and alluring, a symbol of romance, but ultimately pretty ordinary."

You believe them to be rare because of what may be the world's most effective marketing campaign. It all began in 1870, when huge diamond mines were discovered in South Africa. The British financiers who had constructed the mines could not believe their good fortune—in the beginning. As diamonds started to be dragged out by the ton, they started to see they had a problem. The only reason people paid such high prices for diamonds, what made them "precious," was their scarcity. If people realized that there were so many of the things out there, they might become only slightly more pricey than cubic zirconia.

So the diamond investors decided to merge their interests into a single entity that could control production and maintain the illusion that diamonds were rare. Thus was born, in 1888, De Beers Consolidated Mines. At its height it either directly owned or controlled all the diamond mines in southern Africa and also owned diamond trading companies in Europe and Israel. While other commodities, such as gold, fluctuated in response to economic conditions, diamonds have pretty much continued to go up in price every year since the Depression.

But the diamond industry's biggest coup was convincing American couples that no engagement was complete without their product. You probably have a sense that the diamond engagement ring is an ancient tradition. In fact, diamond engagement rings didn't come into vogue until the late nineteenth century, and the custom didn't really take hold until the 1930s.

There were rings of course. Betrothal rings date back to the Romans. Victorians liked to set birthstones in their promissory rings. Diamonds started to accompany wedding proposals after the windfall in the South African mines drove diamond prices down. In other words, they were originally the stone of choice because they were affordable. When prices began to rise, people switched to less expensive alternatives. Beginning in 1919, De Beers experienced a drop in sales that would drag on for twenty years. In order to turn things around they decided they needed to do some serious marketing to convince men and women that their gems were the only acceptable stones for engagements and that they were "forever," by which they meant they should never be resold.

They launched one of history's first product placement and buzz marketing campaigns. De Beers's advertising firm convinced movie stars to wear big diamond rings in public and got the fashion magazines to print stories about the hot new craze. They got the gossip magazines to twitter about the size of the diamond that the dashing motion picture idol gave to his glamorous screen goddess. Between 1938 and 1941, diamond sales went up 55 percent. By 1965, 80 percent of American brides-to-be had diamonds on their engagement rings. As they became an indispensable part of a wedding proposal, the industry's guidelines for the "customary cost" of a ring doubled from one month's salary to two. The average cost of a diamond today is $3,200. What better way to begin your new life together than heavily in debt?

> **Factoid:** The largest seller of diamonds in the United States is Wal-Mart.

Now diamonds are facing a new source of competition—synthetics. Researchers have perfected a chemical process that grows diamonds as pure and almost as big as the best stuff dragged out of an Angolan mine.

"The technology is now at a point that we can grow a more perfect diamond than we can find in nature," said James Butler of the U.S. Naval Research Lab.

The diamond mining companies do not like this at all. De Beers spokeswoman Lynette Gould told *Smithsonian*, "Diamonds are rare and special things with an inherent value that does not exist in factory made synthetics. When people want to celebrate a unique relationship they want a unique diamond, not a three-day-old factory-made stone." If you're going to make a symbolic gesture, be sure it is an expensive one.

Meghan O'Rourke, writing in *Slate* magazine, offers one more reason to forego the diamond. Feminism.

"In an age of equitable marriage the engagement ring is an outmoded commodity," she wrote, "starting with the obvious fact that only the woman gets one. The diamond ring is the site of retrograde fantasies about gender roles."

O'Rourke points out that the boom in diamond engagement ring sales coincided with another change in society. Until the 1930s, jilted fiancés were protected by "Breach of Promise to Marry" laws. To be marriageable you had to be a virgin, but young couples had the same hormones back then as they do now, so a lot of engaged gals let their guards down. As courts began to abolish the legal protections of a lady's honor, diamond sales went up. The rings were a kind of insurance policy. If the guy proposed just to get you into bed, and then dumped you leaving your reputation in tatters, at least you had a nice rock.

"Implicitly, it would seem, a woman's virginity was worth the price of a ring, and varied according to the status of her groom-to-be," wrote O'Rourke. "Virginity is no longer a prerequisite for marriage, nor do the majority of women consider marriageability their prime asset. . . . The engagement ring doesn't fit into this intellectual framework. . . .

Nor is it exactly 'equitable' to demand that a partner shell out a sixth of a year's salary, demonstrating that he can 'provide' for you and a future family, before you agree to marry him."

During his years of poverty the French writer Honore de Balzac lived in an unheated and almost unfurnished garret. On one of the bare walls the writer inscribed the words: "Rosewood paneling with commode," on another, "Gobelin tapestry with Venetian mirror," and in the place of honor over the empty fireplace: "Picture by Raphael."

35

Still Want to Feel Rich? Okay, You're One of the Richest People in the World

....

"If we could all live our lives as resourcefully as people with so little do! Whereas we live in such luxury yet complain about things and moan about things."

—DANNY BOYLE, DIRECTOR OF *SLUMDOG MILLIONAIRE*

Seriously, if you have a toilet to flush you're doing better than one billion people on earth. That is the number of people who do not have a sanitary system of any kind where they live. One third of the planet is that poor. By contrast, by 2005, 95 percent of new U.S. homes had two or more bathrooms and 26 percent had three or more bathrooms.

Having to cancel your Netflix subscription doesn't seem like such a hardship now does it?

If you make $10,787 a year, the U.S. poverty line for an individual, you are in the top 13 percent of wealth in the world. (It has been noted that America is the only country in the world where when you go to get your welfare check there is a parking problem.) If you make the median salary of a U.S. man, $43,460, you are in the top 2.17 percent richest people on the earth. (Source: Globalrichlist.com, which has a cool calculator that allows you to put your wealth in international perspective.)

Things are so good in America that our citizens take it for granted that every person needs a car and that having adult children in the same household as their parents is a sign of immaturity or financial failure. If you're pained by the social stigma that comes with being unable to move out of your mother's basement, remember that it is a luxury to feel this way.* What a grand assumption it is that every adult should have his own home. In Malawi, where the per capita GDP is $600, they're too busy trying to get fed to worry about those kinds of things.

Trying to get by on minimum wage? Think about this: Half of the people on earth survive on less than $2 a day. Embarrassed that you can't afford to buy a house? About 1.1 billion people have inadequate or no housing at all. Wish you could go out to restaurants more? Bear in mind 840 million people are malnourished and 6 million children under the age of five die every year as a result of hunger. Nearly 1.1 billion people in developing countries have inadequate access to water.

Sad that you can't afford a Wii or a Playstation? Remember that nearly 30 percent of the world's population have no electricity. Put another way, the average U.S. citizen in one year uses as much energy as 531 Ethiopians. Concerned about your health care premiums? Contemplate this: diarrhea accounts for an estimated 12,600 deaths each day in children in Asia, Africa, and Latin America.

---

* Incidentally, you know who also lives with her mom in government housing? Michelle Obama.

Having a car to be behind on payments for seems like kind of a blessing, doesn't it?

> **Factoid:** More grain goes to feeding American cows than to feeding all the people of India and China.

While we're putting your situation in perspective, think for a moment about a phrase we've been hearing so much of lately: "in these economic times," and "in times like these."

"It's becoming increasingly difficult to write a news story without using the phrase 'in these economic times.' If only you could buy stock in a cliché," wrote Jeff Bercovici in *Conde Nast Portfolio*. It's almost enough to make you run into the street crying, "We're all doomed!"

So let's take a long, hard look at "these times" by comparing them to life a century ago. "In these tough economic times" you may find yourself counting your pennies a bit more carefully before you go to a grocery store that is filled with shelf after shelf of cheap, safe consumer goods including fresh fruit in or out of season, and all manner of imported items that would have been delicacies to even the wealthiest monarchs of past ages.

You may find that you are stuck forty hours a week in a job that is much less than your ideal. Maybe you have had to endure the indignity of the unemployment line. You may be facing the prospect of trying to survive on little more than a social security check. Maybe you've been forced to downsize from a larger house to a smaller one, from a better neighborhood to a worse one, from a home you own to an apartment. If worse comes to worst, you might find yourself relying on welfare or food stamps.

Now compare your situation with that of the average Joe in the mid-1800s. Without social benefits or unions (only 3.5 percent of the workforce was unionized by 1900), you would be forced to endure whatever your boss could dish out—and he could dish out a lot! Chances are, no matter how bad your twenty-first-century job is, you are not working twelve-hour shifts in a 117-degree factory, seven days a week. Working men were frequently injured on the job; they lost limbs; they were crushed and poisoned. And when they were, the boss would send them on their way with no workers' compensation and no sense of responsibility. Women who packed soap in sweatshops were exposed to soda that ate away at their fingers. Flower packers were slowly poisoned by the arsenic that was added to bring out vivid colors.

Before child labor laws, you might end up on a factory floor or deep in a mine shaft when you'd barely mastered walking. Young mine workers, exposed to poisonous dust and constant danger, earned 25 cents for a 12–14 hour day in the dark. And forget about retirement. In the good old days, workers had no social security or pensions, and many kept working twelve hours a day until they could no longer stand rather than risk slow starvation.

Perhaps you were paid in company scrip that was only good at the inflated company store, this in a time when food costs in the best case already accounted for 50 percent of the typical salary. Farmers fared barely better. In the 1880s, roughly 40 percent of farmers were tenants. They didn't own the house or the land.

Urban living was fraught with perils as overcrowded wooden tenements began to rise up. Heated by coal stoves, they were full of pollution and soot. Between 1868 an 1875 an estimated 500,000—about half the New York City population—lived in slums, with as many as eight people sharing a living room of ten by twelve feet and a bedroom of six by eight feet. One tenement was packed with 101 adults and 91 children. And the practice of financially penalizing the poor was alive and well. The rent per square foot of squalor was actually 25–35 percent more per foot than that of the fashionable uptown apartments.

But a lack of personal space was the least of a nineteenth-century worker's worries. Those overcrowded wooden buildings were fire traps. Between 1870 and 1906 four American cities—Chicago, Boston, Baltimore, and San Francisco—burned to the ground.

Pigs wandered New York City streets feeding off piles of refuse tossed out of windows. The city's poor relied on the garbage-fed animals for their supper. Antibiotics did not come into use until well into the twentieth century, and illnesses that are considered mild inconveniences today were then killers. The filth and crowding led to mass epidemics of cholera and yellow fever. During one of the worst outbreaks, one New York City tenement recorded a fatality rate of 20 percent. *Hot Corn*, a newspaper of the time, described the conditions: "Saturate your handkerchief with camphor so that you can endure the horrid stench, and enter. Grope your way through the long narrow passage—turn up to the right, up the dark and dangerous stairs; be careful where you place your foot around the lower step, or in the corners of the broad stairs, for it is more than shoe-mouth deep of steaming filth."

It has been estimated that 80 billion modern humans have walked the earth since Homo sapiens started walking erect. Gregg Easterbook, author of *The Progress Paradox,* points out that this means people living at middle class standards or above in the United States or the European Union now live better than 99.4 *percent of the human beings who ever existed.*

How do you feel about "these economic times" now? The fact of the matter is, there is hardly a better time in history to be alive. If you don't have a fortune, thank your lucky stars that you live in "times like these."

"In times like these, it helps to recall there have always been times like these."

—PAUL HARVEY, AMERICAN RADIO BROADCASTER

Resources

Free Stuff

FreeCycle.org: This nonprofit organization, with a mission to help the environment by not cluttering landfills, matches people who want to give away items with people in the same city who want them.

Craigslist.com: Craigslist has categories for free stuff and barter. Look up your metropolitan area.

Freesamplesite.com: A bulletin board where people post information on free product samples, coupons, discounts, and sweepstakes.

Free Food

Angelfoodministries.com: Through a network of churches, you can purchase food at very low cost. There is no income requirement; anyone can participate.

Freejunkfood.blogspot.com: Not a source for free food, but a blog maintained by a freegan with a regular catalog of his Dumpster-dive finds and recipes for meals made from foraged foodstuffs.

FreeBirthdayTreats.com: Find out which restaurants give free or discounted meals or services to people on their birthdays.

Kidsmealdeals.com: Check this site to find out where kids eat for free with a paying adult. Register with your zip code and get a list of local offers.

Free Lodging

HomeExchange.com: Want to travel but don't want to pay for a hotel room? You can swap homes with people across the country and world. Or you can host each other as guests.

Free Credit Reports

Creditkarma.com: Check your credit score for free. Really.

Free Software

Giveawayoftheday.com: Each day this site offers licensed software (the license can be activated only within the twenty-four-hour period) that would otherwise have to be purchased.

Openoffice.org: Free open source word processing and productivity suite.

Techsupportalert.com: Home of Gizmo's Best Ever Freeware with reviews and links to the best free software, including free anti-virus programs.

Free Legal and Business Advice

Score.org: Retired business executives offer free advice and mentoring to help small businesses.

Avvo.com: Get free legal advice from an attorney.

Mental Health/Emotional Support

Elderwisdomcircle.org: Senior citizens volunteer and provide confidential, personal, and compassionate advice by e-mail.

Debtorsanonymous.org: Debtors Anonymous is a twelve-step support group to provide support and help others recover from compulsive debting.

Samaritans.org: Samaritans provides free confidential non-judgmental emotional support, twenty-four hours a day by telephone and e-mail for people who are experiencing feelings of distress or despair, including those that could lead to suicide.

Barter

Barterquest.com. Exchange site where members can post their wants and needs.

Nate.org: The National Association of Trade Exchanges is an organization that allows businesses to trade goods and services using trade credits.

Swapstyle.com: Trade clothes, accessories, shoes, or unused beauty products.

Bookmooch.com: Swap books.

Titletrader.com: Trade books, CDs and DVDs.

Barter.net: A directory of barter group by state.

Trashbank.com: Barter, swap, trade, or sell your item or service.

Swapathome.com: Tries to eliminate the difficulty of matching items to trade with items wanted by swapping for coupons that can be traded for any item.

Swapsimple.com: Trade books, DVDs, and games.

Swaptreasures.com: Swap, barter, buy, or sell.

Libraries

Nces.ed.gov/surveys/libraries/librarysearch: Find a library near you using a searchable database.

Thrift Shopping

Thethriftshopper.com: A directory of thrift shopping, searchable by address or zip code.

Estatesales.net: Find estate sales in your area and sign up to receive e-mail notification of upcoming sales.

Yardsalequeen.com: Tips for holding and shopping at yard sales.

Unclaimedbaggage.com: These huge thrift stores, located in Southern states, sell lost airline luggage. The website offers a virtual tour and e-mail sign up.

Bibliography

Amen, Daniel. *Sex on the Brain*. New York: Random House, 2008.

Anielski, Mark. *The Economics of Happiness*. Gabriola Island, Canada: New Society Publishers, 2007.

Arnst, Catherine. "Study Links Medical Costs and Personal Bankruptcy," *Business Week*, June 4, 2009.

Augst, Thomas. "Introduction: American Libraries and Agencies of Culture," *American Studies* 42, no. 3, 2000.

Ayan, Steve J. and Iris Tajuana Calliess. "Abnormal as Norm." *Scientific American*, March 24, 2005.

Bageant, Joe. *Deer Hunting with Jesus: Dispatches from America's Class War*. New York: Crown Publishing, 2007.

Barrow, Becky. "Money Worries Can Bankrupt Your Love Life." *Daily Mail*, January 20, 2006.

Beiler, Ryan. "The Tao of Dumpster Diving." *Sojourners Magazine*, May 2006.

Blakenhorn, David. *Thrift: A Cyclopedia*. West Conshohocken, PA: Templeton Foundation Press, 2008.

Bodies, Rest and Motion (DVD Commentary). Dir. Micheal Steinberg. Pref. Phoebe Cates, Bridget Fonda, Tim Roth, Eric Stoltz. DVD. New Line Home Entertainment, 1993.

Boily, David. "Man Uses a Paper Clip to Barter for a House." *USA Today*, April 16, 2006.

Boren, James H. *Fuzzify*. McLean, VA: EPM Publications, 1982.

Borer, Shane. "Could You Collect More in a Panther Outfit?" *CFO Snafu*, October 16, 2008.

Boser, Ulrich. "Diamonds on Demand." *Smithsonian*, June 2008.

Boslet, Mark. "Our Guilty Gallons: Bottled Water's Impact on Environment." *San Jose Mercury News*, December 16, 2007.

Bowden, Jonny. *The 150 Healthiest Foods on Earth*. Beverly, MA: Fair Winds, 2007.

Brafman, Ori and Rom Brafman. *Sway: The Irresistible Pull of Irrational Behavior*. New York: Doubleday, 2008.

Breen, Bill. "The 6 Myths of Creativity." *Fast Company*, December 19, 2007.

Britten, Fleur. "Where Old Clothes Go to Die." *Sunday Times*, May 25, 2008.

Brock, Alice. *Alice's Restaurant Cookbook*. New York: Random House, 1969.

Bud, Mike et al. *Consuming Environments: Television and Commercial Culture*. New Brunswick, NJ: Rutgers University Press, 1999.

Burkeman, Oliver. "This Column Will Change Your Life." *Guardian*, May 10, 2008.

Burnham, Terry and Jay Phelan. *Mean Genes*. New York: Perseus Publishing, 2000.

Callahan, David. *The Cheating Culture*. New York: Harcourt, 2004.

Cassingham, Randy. *This is True: Cost of Being Poor Rising*. Pamphlet. Boulder, CO: Freelance Communications, 2000.

———. *This is True: Deputy Kills Man with Hammer*. Pamphlet. Boulder, CO; Freelance Communications, 1999.

Cialdini, Robert B. *Influence: Science and Practice*. Boston: Allyn and Bacon, 2001.

Coltrane, Scott. *Gender and Families*. Lanham, MA: Altamira Press, 2000.

Conan, Neal. "Analysis: Why People Worry and How to Deal with it." *Talk of the Nation* (National Public Radio), June 10, 2002.

Consumersunion.org. (Publisher of Consumer Reports).

Cox, Harvey. "The Market as God." *Atlantic Monthly*, March 1999.

D'Alessandro, David and Michele Owens. *Brand Warfare: 10 Rules for Building the Killer Brand*. New York: McGraw Hill, 2002.

"Daydream Achievers." *MX Sydney*, May 13, 2009.

Deegan, Gordon. "Burnout Priests." *The Mirror*, February 7, 2002.

DeGraaf, John et al. *Affluenza*. San Francisco: Berrett-Koehler Publishers, 2001.

De Botton, Alain. *The Consolations of Philosophy*. New York: Vintage, 2000.

———. *How Proust Can Change Your Life*. New York: Vintage, 1997.

———. *Status Anxiety*. New York: Vintage, 2005.

Dieu est Americain/God is American. DVD. Palladium Productions, 2007.

Duany, Andrés et al. *Suburban Nation*. New York: North Point Press, 2000.

Easterbrook, Gregg. *The Progress Paradox*. New York: Random House, 2003.

Eckersley, Richard (director and fellow, Australia 21 Ltd) Telephone interview by author. May 4, 2009.

———. "The politics of happiness." *Living Now*, March 2007.

Epstein, Edward Jay. "Have You Ever Tried to Sell a Diamond?" *The Atlantic*, February 1982.

Fischman, Wendy et al. *Making Good: How Young People Cope with Moral Dilemmas at Work*. Cambridge, MA: Harvard University Press, 2004.

Fox, Michael J. *Lucky Man*. New York: Hyperion, 2003.

Frank, Robert H. *Falling Behind*. Los Angeles: University of California Press, 2007.

"From Paperclip to House in 14 Trades," *CBC News*, July 7, 2006.

Gardner, John. "Do You Have What it Takes to Become a Novelist?" *Esquire,* April 1983.

Gilbert, Daniel. *Stumbling on Happiness*. New York: Alfred A. Knopf, 2006.

Gladwell, Malcolm. "The Uses of Adversity." *The New Yorker*, November 10, 2008.

Glausiusz, Josie. "Devoted to Distraction." *Psychology Today*, March/April 2009.

Goldberg, M. Hirsch. *The Complete Book of Greed*. New York: William Morrow and Company, 1994.

Gore, Al. *The Assault on Reason*. New York: Penguin, 2007.

Grobman, Paul. *Vital Statistics*. New York: Plume, 2005.

Grohol, John M. "Money Can Change Your Behavior toward Others." *Pysch Central*, July 9, 2008.

Gunther, Marc. "The Amazing Freecycle Story." *CNN Money*, July 13, 2007.

Guthrie, Arlo (musician). Interview by author. Pittsfield, MA, April 13, 1999.

Hanh, Tich Nhat. *Living Buddha, Living Christ*. New York: Riverhead Books, 1995.

Havel, Vaclav. *The Power of the Powerless*. New York: M.E. Sharpe., Inc, 1985.

Hay, Peter. *The Book of Business Anecdotes*. New York: Wings Books, 1988.

Hayasaki, Erika. "Free-lunch Foragers." *Los Angeles Times*, September 11, 2007.

Hodgson, Godfrey. *The Myth of American Exceptionalism*. New Haven, CT: Yale University Press, 2009.

Hoff, Al. *Thrift Score*. New York: Harper Perennial, 1997.

Honore, Carl. *In Praise of Slowness*. New York: Harper Collins, 2004.

Huber, Cheri. *There is Nothing Wrong with You.* Mountain View, CA: Keep it Simple Books, 1993.

Hunter, Jennifer (high school teacher). E-mail correspondence with author. May 12, 2009.

Hyman, Dick. *Cockeyed Americana.* Brattleboro, VT: Stephen Greene Press, 1972.

Ivanko, John and Lisa Kivirst. "Making a Life." *E Magazine*, July/August, 2008.

Jones, Chris (filmmaker). Telephone interview by author. April 3, 2009.

Jones, Roland Gary. *They Went Broke?!* New York: Gramercy, 2004.

Kaufman, Leslie. "Mr. Whipple Left it Out." *New York Times*, February 26, 2009.

Kazmann, Reena. "Finding Alternatives to the Trash Pile." *Eco-Artware.com*, Spring/Summer 2001.

Kunstler, James. *Geography of Nowhere.* New York: Free Press, 2004.

Lackey, Mike. "Now We've Got to Worry About Worrying, Too." *The Lima News*, May 2, 2007.

Lane, Robert E. *The Loss of Happiness in Market Democracies.* New Haven, CT: Yale University Press, 2000.

Lee, Laura. *100 Most Dangerous Things in Everyday Life and What You Can Do About Them.* New York: Broadway Books, 2004.

———. *Pocket Encyclopedia of Aggravation.* New York: Black Dog and Leventhal, 2001.

Lennon, John. "Ridin' the Rails: The Place of the Passenger and the Space of the Hobo." *Americana: The Journal of American Popular Culture*, Fall 2004.

Levine, Daniel S. *Disgruntled: The Darker Side of the World of Work.* New York: Berkeley Boulevard Books, 1998.

Littlefield, Bruce. *Garage Sale America.* New York: Harper Collins, 2007.

Loewen, James W. *Lies My Teacher Told Me.* New York: The New Press, 1995.

Longacre, Doris Janzen. *Living More with Less.* Scottsdale, PA: Herald Press, 1980.

Lord, John et al. *Beacon Lights of History: The Middle Ages.* Boston: Fords, Howard and Hulburt, 1885.

Lutz, Tom. *Doing Nothing.* New York: MacMillan, 2007.

Marco, Meghann. "20% of Americans Fear They'll Never Escape Credit Card Debt." *The Consumerist*, June 6, 2007.

Martin-Jordan, Richard. (French filmmaker). E-mail correspondence with author, June 1, 2009.

"The Maven's Word of the Day." www.randomhouse.com/word. August 31, 2000.

McDaniel, Jay. *Living from the Center: Spirituality in an Age of Consumerism*. St. Louis, MO: Chalice Press, 2000.

McGeehan, Patrick. "Soaring Interest Compounds Credit Card Pain for Millions." *New York Times*, November 21, 2004.

"Michael Jackson Flunked his Credit Report." *TMZ*, August 28, 2009.

Montagne, Rene. "The Rise and Fall of the Chilean Sea Bass." *Morning Edition*, National Public Radio, August 28, 2006.

Montano, Linda M. *Performance Artists Talking in the Eighties*. Los Angeles: University of California Press, 2000.

Morrison, Terri et al. *Kiss, Bow or Shake Hands*. Holbrook, MA: Adams Media, 1994.

Moses, Barbara. *Women Confidential*. New York: Marlowe and Company, 2006.

Moskowitz, Jennifer. "The Cultural Myth of the Cowboy, or, How the West Was Won." *Americana: The Journal of American Popular Culture*, Spring 2006.

Moss, Jon. Video interview. http://www.youtube.com/watch?v=sBdsAlgXv0U. Accessed: May 3, 2009.

Neugarten, Bernice Levin. *Middle Age and Aging: A Reader in Social Psychology*. Chicago: University of Chicago Press, 1968.

Newell, Iris. *Generation Deluxe*. Toronto: Dundurn Press, 2004.

O'Rourke, Meghan. "Diamonds Are a Girl's Worst Friend." *Slate*, June 11, 2007.

Offil, Jenny and Elissa Schappell, eds. *Money Changes Everything*. New York: Doubleday, 2007.

Oliver, Rachel. "All About Food Waste." *CNN.com*, January 22, 2008.

Petry, Ray C. *Francis of Assisi: Apostle of Poverty*. New York: AMS Press, 1964.

Poet, J. "Sliding Into a Unique Niche." *San Francisco Chronicle*, September 3, 2006.

Pravato, Kira Paulli. "Overfishing Threatens European Bluefin Tuna." *Eurekalert*, November 7, 2008.

Precker, Michael. "Witch Casts Aside Job Uncertainty with Spellbinding Book." *Dallas Morning News*, November 20, 2001.

"The Public View." *Gainesville Sun*, September 11, 2008.

Putnam, Robert D. *Bowling Alone*. New York: Simon and Schuster, 2000.

Rathje, William and Cullen Murphy. *Rubbish! The Archaeology of Garbage*. New York: Harper Collins, 1992.

Revior, Paul. "We Worry for Two Hours a Day." *Daily Mail,* December 30, 2008.

Robinson, John P. and Geoffrey Godbey. *Time for Life: The Surprising Ways Americans Use Their Time.* University Park, PA: Pennsylvania State University Press, 1997.

Roger, Robin. "Diamond Dilemma: Be Wary of Blood Diamonds." *Bradenton Herald,* July 30, 2006.

Rogers, Heather. *Gone Tomorrow: The Hidden Life of Garbage*. New York: W.W. Norton, 2005.

Rowbotham, Michael. *The Grip of Death: A Study of Modern Money, Debt Slavery and Destructive Economics*. Charlbury, UK: 1998.

Ryan, Pam and Denise Koufogiannakis. "Librarianship and the Culture of Busy." *Partnership: the Canadian Journal of Library and Information Practice and Research*, Vol 2, No 1, 2007.

Sammler-Michael, Scott. "Free Market Theology Exposed." Sermon: Presented at the Accotink Unitarian Universalist Church, January 11, 2009. (http://www.accotinkuuc.org/Free%20Market%20Theology%20Exposed.pdf)

Sanchez, Anita. *The Teeth of the Lion*. Blacksburg, VA: The McDonald and Woodward Publishing Company, 2006.

Sandage, Scott. *Born Losers*. Cambridge, MA: Harvard University Press, 2005.

Scoblionkov, Deborah. "Garbage In, Art Out." *Philadelphia City Paper*, May 21-28, 1998.

Scurlock, James D. *Maxed Out: Hard Times, Easy Credit and the Era of Predatory Lenders*. New York: Scribner, 2007.

Serres, Chris. "Do Africa's Wars Dim Glitter of Diamonds?" *Star Tribune* (Minneapolis, MN), December 7, 2006.

Shenkman, Richard and Kurt Reigner. *One-Night Stands with American History*. New York: Quill, 1982.

Shepherd, Chuck. "News of the Weird." *Inside Tucson Business*, November 6, 2004.

Shorris, Earl. "Foreclosed Dream in Detroit." *The Nation*, September 24, 1983.

Simmons, Philip. *Learning to Fall*. New York: Bantam, 2000.

Slade, Giles. *Made to Break: Technology and Obsolescence in America*. Boston, MA: Harvard University Press, 2006.

Slater, Philip. *The Pursuit of Lonliness*. Boston, MA: Beacon Press, 1970.

"Smoke, mirrors . . . and how a handful of missed mortgage payments started the global financial crisis." *Sunday Herald*, October 4, 2008.

"Sneaky Manufacturers Shrink Packaging, While Keeping Prices the Same." *Center for Media and Democracy*, www.prwatch.org. Accessed: November 19, 2008.

"Social vs. Financial Thinking." *Psyblog*: http://www.spring.org.uk/2008/04/social-versus-financial-thinking-when.php. Accessed: May 20, 2009.

Stiles, Paul. *Is the American Dream Killing You?* New York: Harper Collins, 2005.

Stokes, Patricia. *Creativity from Constraints*. New York: Springer Publishing, 2006.

Strasser, Susan. *Waste and Want*. New York: Metropolitan Books, 1999.

Stout, David. "Senate Passes Bill to Restrict Credit Card Practices." *New York Times*, May 19, 2009.

Sullivan, Bob. *Gotcha Capitalism*. New York: Ballantine, 2007.

Swaminathan, Nikhil, "For the Brain, Cash is Good, Status is Better," *Scientific American*, April 24, 2008.

Tennent, Sarah. "Pros and Cons of Water-Only Hair Washing." *Suite 101*, June 22, 2008.

Thomas, Dana. *Deluxe: How Luxury Lost its Luster*. New York: Penguin, 2007.

"Tip of the Day: Make Your Own Kitty Litter." *Allie's Answers*, http://alliesanswers.com/tip-of-the-day/tip-of-the-day-make-your-own-kitty-litter/1044. Accessed May 3, 2009.

Twenge, Jean M. *Generation Me*. New York: Free Press, 2006.

Twist, Lynne. *The Soul of Money*. New York: W.W. Norton, 2003.

Twitchell, James B. *Branded Nation*. New York: Simon and Schuster, 2004.

———. *Shopping for God*. New York: Simon and Scheuster, 2007.

U.S. Public Interest Research Group. http://www.uspirg.org/

Upton, Lavon. "Libraries Booming In Recession." *Oakland Press*, May 3, 2009.

Useem, Jerry et al. "One Nation Under Wal-Mart." *Fortune*, March 3, 2003.

Wallace, Mike. "Hilary Swank: Oscar Gold." *CBS Evening News*, March 2, 2005.

Wasserman, Dale. *The Impossible Musical*. New York: Applause Books, 2003.

Wharton, Edith. *The House of Mirth*. New York: Penguin Books, 2000.

Whybrow, Peter. *American Mania: When More is Not Enough*. New York: Norton, 2005.

Whyllie, Irvin G. *The Self Made Man in America: The Myth of Rags to Riches*. Toronto: MacMillan, 1954.

Wilson, Eric G. *Against Happiness*. New York: Farrar, Straus, Giroux, 2008.

Winerpip, Michael. "Our Towns; Where the Rich Find Comfort in Each Other." *The New York Times*, March 1, 1988.

Winokur, Jon. *The Rich Are Different*. New York: Pantheon Books, 1996.

Wiseman, Thomas. *The Money Motive*. New York: Random House, 1974.

Wood, Wendy-Jo et al. "People's Perceptions of Women's and Men's Worry about Life Issues." *Sex Roles*: Vol. 53, Issue 7/8, October, 2005.

Yeager, Jeff. *The Ultimate Cheapskate's Road Map to True Riches*. New York: Broadway Books, 2007.

Zweig, Jason. *Your Money and Your Brain*. New York: Simon and Schuster, 2007.

Zweig, Michael. *Working Class Majority*. Ithaca, NY: Cornell University Press, 2000.